CREATIVITY IN SMALL GROUPS

D0882366

CREATIVITY
IN
SMALL
GROUPS

A. Paul Hare

SAGE PUBLICATIONS
Beverly Hills / London / New Delhi

Copyright © 1982 by Sage Publications, Inc.

For information address:

SAGE Publications, Inc.
275 South Beverly Drive
Beverly Hills, California 90212

SAGE Publications India Pvt. Ltd.
C-236 Defence Colony
New Delhi 110 024, India

SAGE Publications Ltd
28 Banner Street
London EC1Y 8QE, England

Printed in the United States of America

Library of Congress Cataloging in Publication Data

Hare, A. Paul (Alexander Paul), 1923-
    Creativity in small groups.
    Bibliography: p.
    Includes indexes.
    1. Small groups. 2. Social interaction.
3. Creative ability. 4. Problem-solving. I. Title.
HM133.H359   302.3'4   81-13583
ISBN 0-8039-1712-0   AACR2
ISBN 0-8039-1713-9 (pbk.)

THIRD PRINTING, 1984   LK 12·21·84

CONTENTS

Acknowledgments

In common with other forms of communication this book has two principal aspects, *content* and *process*. On the content side I am indebted to those persons who introduced me to the four theoretical perspectives that I use and to the possibility of applying them to the analysis of creativity in small groups. Andrew Effrat was the person who initially made many of the mysteries of the functional approach clear to me and provided me with the first basic category system. Since then he has, perhaps wisely, actively refrained from suggesting any particular path to follow in using the categories. For my view of the three and four dimensional approach to the analysis of interpersonal behavior, I might be considered to be standing on the shoulders of R. Freed Bales and Arthur S. Couch. However it feels more like clinging to their backs since I seem to be viewing groups from about the same elevation, but with a slightly different perspective. Although I knew J. L. Moreno and had had several pleasant conversations with him about the origins of his interest in psychodrama, it was not until after his death that I became involved directly with psychodrama when in 1976 I accompanied my wife June to sessions at the Moreno Institute in Beacon, New York, where she was training to become a psychodrama director. This has been followed by other direct experiences at the Moreno Institute and elsewhere. Zerka Moreno was especially helpful in selecting materials for my short biography of J. L. Moreno in the *International Encyclopedia of Social Science*. Since I happened to be around Harvard University when George Homans returned from his year at the Harvard Business School, full of enthusiasm for the possibilities of applying economic exchange theory to other forms of social behavior, I had a rather early introduction to this approach. However it was not until 1975, when John Mueller worked with me for a brief period as a research assistant, that I was able to use the approach in any detailed way.

For introducing me to the possibilities of applying the four perspectives to the study of creativity, I have Ken Jubber to thank. Fortunately for me, Ken had chosen the Herculean task of bringing together information from a variety of fields on the subject of "the human stock of knowledge." In the final version of his doctoral thesis, Ken had to settle for a less ambitious goal, but in the course of my duties as his thesis advisor at the University of Cape Town, I had to read and comment on early drafts of chapters. It was then that I recognized that the steps in group problem-solving and in the creative process were essentially the same and that all of the insights of group dynamics could be applied to the analysis of creativity in groups.

There are three types of processes that have been involved in bringing this volume to publication. The first is a process of formal research, the second a process of social action, and the last a process of book manufacturing. For my involvement in the process of formal research on nonviolent direct action in the United States in the late 1960s and early 1970s I am indebted to the National Institute of Mental Health which provided a substantial grant to support a research team composed of persons from the nonviolent movement and from academic halls. Among those who made major contributions to the team effort were Herb Blumberg, Charles Walker, Bert Kritzer, Dean Peabody, Dean MacCannell, Sid Waldman, and Julie Latané. Some of the case material presented in this volume is a result of our collaboration in that research project. Additional insight into creative group process was gained in social action as part of a nonviolent response to some crisis or some continuing conflict. Some of the same people who joined me in research were also involved in one or more of the action projects that are mentioned briefly in this volume or that provided some of the background experience. These actions took place in the mainland of the United States, Puerto Rico, Culebra, Cyprus, India, and South Africa. Also on the action side, the activities of Narayan Desai, one of the leaders of the present day Gandhian Movement in India, have been a constant source of inspiration. The model he provided through the work of the Shanti Sena (Peace Brigade) in various crises in India has provided guidelines for activity in many other situations.

Moving finally to the process of book manufacture, I am indebted in the first instance to the students at Ben-Gurion University who absorbed the contents of early draft chapters and demonstrated in their own research that the various perspectives could be used to illuminate the activities of small groups in Israel. Next I wish to thank the three persons who read the manuscript in draft form: Paul Shane for his most constructive criticisms concerning the organization of the book, Haim Murantz for calling my attention to the philosophical implications of some of the statements that I was making, and my wife June (Rabson Hare) for a detailed reading of the text that included suggestions for the spelling of words (where her version was closer to truth) and the placement of commas (where I was inclined to let the sentences run on). While the writing was in progress, June spent more than her share of hours with Andrew, two years, and Simon, five years, while I was closeted (literally) at the office.

It should be apparent that many groups have been involved over a number of years in providing material for this volume. It is because I believe that so much has been accomplished through the cooperation of the members of these groups that I have tried to pass on some of the experience in this volume. I wish to thank again all those I have mentioned here and the many more who will see their work reflected in these pages. Without the experience with them in groups, I would be less of an individual.

A. Paul Hare

Introduction

"There is nothing new under the sun."
Ecclesiastes 1:9

What does it mean that "there is nothing new under the sun?" Does it mean that for new things we should look under the moon? That is part of the answer, since when we look under the sun we see things in familiar ways. When we look at them by moonlight the outlines may be blurred, perspective may vanish, or other distinctions may be lost. Some things that by day may appear different, by night may appear the same. Thus by moonlight there is the possibility of a "creative shift" in our vision that may make it possible to see things in new relationships and thus lead to some new understanding or some new physical creation.

If there is nothing new under the sun, does it really mean that everything was there before? That is also part of the answer. Light was bending on its way from distant stars for many years before Einstein discovered it. He did not create any new laws for the universe but he did have the ability to break from accepted patterns of thought and to be open to the realization of the ways in which the laws actually functioned.

Although everything that we will have to work with may indeed be present in some form under the sun, we have apparently not yet realized all the potential for combinations and permutations of our physical and social resources. Whether one is more concerned about the destructive forces of human beings or the destructive forces in nature, one can find a motivation for using one's creative talents to ward off disaster and to make everyday living a fuller, more humane experience.

Some social scientists have focused on the personality characteristics and thought processes of individuals who are known to be especially creative. Other have been more interested in the possibilities for creativity in everyday living. Although this research will be reviewed briefly in the present volume, the focus here will be on how sets of individuals in small groups can combine together for maximum creativity. However, it turns out that the steps in the creative process are essentially the same as the steps in ordinary problem solving. The difference lies in the degree of originality of the product. Thus, before we look at creative groups it is well to understand the basic characteristics of problem-solving groups. Since problem-solving groups have processes and structures that are similar to other types of groups that are not "problem oriented" it is helpful to look at the general characteristics of small groups. For this we need some theoretical perspectives and some methods of analysis.

Having backed off sufficiently from the problem of "creativity" in groups to gain additional perspective, we are now ready to begin this book. The book is divided into three parts. The first part of four chapters introduces four theoretical perspectives and category systems for applying the perspectives. The *functional perspective* is based on the four functions (AGIL) theory of Parsons and his colleagues with a category system proposed by Effrat. The perspective of *four dimensions of interaction* has been developed from the contributions of social-psychologists—including Chapple, Leary, Couch, and Bales—who have sought to identify basic dimensions of interaction process. The method of *dramaturgical analysis* is based on the psychodramatic theory of Moreno. The propositions in *exchange analysis* are drawn from the work of Thibaut and Kelley, Homans, Blau, and others, and the category system is an extension of the work of Longabaugh.

All four of the systems are related. The categories for dramaturgical and exchange analysis are extensions and variations of the functional categories and the four dimensions of interaction. The four systems can be used together to provide one category system with emphasis on each of the four functional (AGIL) sectors. In exchange analysis the focus is on the economic processes in a group (A), in functional analysis on the type of group task (G), in the four dimensions on the roles and interrelations of members (I), and in dramaturgical analysis in the images that can provide the overall meaning of the group behavior (L).

Part II, also of four chapters, provides an analysis of some aspects of group process and structure in terms of one or more of the four perspectives from Part I. In Chapter 5 on group development, there is a summary of the theories of Tuckman, Mann, and Shambaugh, followed by some hypotheses concerning group development based on functional theory. In Chapter 6 on social control, brief accounts are given of the experiments on conformity of Asch and Milgram and the theories of Jahoda and Kellman. A summary analysis is based on functional theory. An overview of sociometric research is given in Chapter 7 on interpersonal choice, and a description of types of leader and member roles from the functional and four dimensional perspectives in Chapter 8.

Part III contains two chapters. Chapter 9 compares individual and group problem-solving with special attention to differences in patterns of interaction associated with group size. The method of "consensus" is described in detail as a way of solving problems in large groups that preserves the advantages of small groups. The analysis of individual and group creativity in the final chapter is summarized in a "flow chart" of steps involved in the process of creative problem solving with groups.

Each chapter includes one or more examples of the application of the perspective of the chapter to the analysis of behavior in laboratory or natural groups. Some of the examples are the result of observations made between 1969 and 1973 while I was principal investigator of a grant from the National Institute of Mental Health (U.S.) for the study of the nonviolent direct action that was much in evidence in the street and on the university campuses in the United States during those years. For a brief period of time we actually had two multidisciplinary research teams of five persons each observing demonstrations. Four of them were trained to observe from the four perspectives described in this volume (that is, AGIL, 4-d, dramaturgical, and exchange). The fifth person recorded the action with movie camera and tape recorder. However we were never successful in bringing all the perspectives to bear on the same case as we had hoped. This was partly the result of the fact that the exchange and dramaturgical category systems had not been developed to the same state as they are at present.

There are three aspects of any science: the method, the point of view, and the application. The three parts of this book emphasize each of these aspects in turn. Part I is written as a manual for the group observer. Four category systems are presented, together with instructions on how to use them, and illustrations of their use. Part II is written for the theorist who wishes to have a framework for understanding process and structure in small groups. Part III is written for the applied scientist who wishes to organize or help groups to be more creative in their problem-solving, especially with social problems.

This is not the whole story. There are other ways that one might bring together information about social interaction in small groups. Since I have been involved in several of these projects, the present volume might best be seen as part of a set, although it does try to weave together many of the threads that are present in the other works.

The reader who is interested in a short introduction to the field with an emphasis on some of the classic studies may wish to read *The Small Group* (Olmsted and Hare, 1978). The reader who is interested in a collection of articles by sociologists and psychologists who have specialized in the study of interpersonal behavior might consult *Small Groups: Studies in Social Interaction* (Hare, Borgatta, and Bales, 1965) for the period up to 1964 and *Small Groups and Social Interaction* (Blumberg, Hare, Kent, and Davies, 1982) for the period from 1965 through 1981. An extensive review of research results is provided in the *Handbook of Small Group*

Research (Hare, 1976b). This last source in particular is recommended for the reader who wishes more documentation concerning the generalizations made in the present text, in some cases without references to specific studies. Finally, for those readers interested in the application of these social-psychological perspectives in the analysis of nonviolent action there are three volumes, all by Hare and Blumberg: *Nonviolent Direct Action* (1968), *Liberation Without Violence: A Third Part Approach* (1977), and *A Search for Peace and Justice: Reflections of Michael Scott* (1980).

Three Schools: Group Dynamics, Sociometry, and Small Groups

If this book had been written in the early 1900s the title could have been simply "creativity" since there was some question as to whether the "group" actually existed. The debate involved the concept of the "group mind." Did groups have a mind in the same way that individuals have a mind that governs their behavior? Thus Deutsch (1954) notes that when Kurt Lewin, one of the first social-psychologists to promote the study of "group dynamics," introduced terms like "group atmosphere" and "group goals" to place the emphasis squarely on the group as a phenomenon, his concepts were considered nonscientific or mystical by some. Although Lewin's research and theory was not limited to group dynamics, Deutsch suggests that one of Lewin's major contributions was to make the concept of "group" acceptable to psychologists.

Lewin was also responsible for introducing the applied side of group dynamics in the form of training groups where leaders in education, business, and other fields could learn the principles of democratic group leadership and problem-solving (Marrow, 1969). Although the emphasis in the first workshop was on the "task" side of interaction in groups, by the second workshop both staff and students discovered that the social-emotional relations in the group (the "interpersonal underworld" according to Schutz [1958]) was equally important, if not more so (Benne, 1964).

Thus, from the beginnings of the "group dynamics" movement there has been an interest in two aspects of social interaction in small groups: the problem-solving side and the interpersonal side. For example, Bion (1961) emphasized this dichotomy. Drawing on his experiences in group therapy, he noted that in any group there is always some level of *work* going on with an undercurrent of some *emotional state*. Bion distinguished three emotional "cultures": Fight or flight, pairing, and dependency. When the existence of the group was threatened members would be moved to "fight or flight," when they wanted the warmth and support of a more intimate relationship they would pair off, and when they felt especially weak and vulnerable they would express their dependency on the leader.

In contrast to Lewin who emphasized the group, Moreno approached the theory and application of the process of social interaction from the point of view of the individual. Moreno had several things in common with Lewin. Both had left Europe for America to escape Hitler's authoritarianism and to work in a more "democratic" climate that was supportive of their ideals. Both wanted to use their knowledge of social psychology to bring about significant changes in society. However Moreno lived for 82 years, until 1974, whereas Lewin died in 1947 at the age of 57, so that Moreno had the opportunity to try out personally many of the ideas that he set forth in his magnum opus *Who Shall Survive?* (1953). Moreno described his book as "the new bible." "It is a bible for social conduct, for human societies," he wrote. "It has more ideas packed in one book than a whole generation of books" (Moreno, 1953: 66). Even if Moreno had been a fairly modest man, others would have acknowledged that he contributed many creative ideas to the study of groups and the application of group dynamics (Hare, 1979).

Two of Moreno's major contributions have to do with the introduction of "sociometry" as a way of measuring and depicting interpersonal attraction in groups and "psychodrama" as a method of group therapy, designed as "social atom" repair work. A "sociometric" question, according to Moreno, was one in which you would ask members of a group to both choose and reject other members whom they would like (or not like) to work with, play with, or whatever, with a particular criterion for selection in mind. After the "test" the group should be restructured to place together those persons who had chosen each other. This would have the effect of surrounding each individual with a "social atom" of mutual choices, persons who could be expected to be supportive and facilitate creativity.

Thus Moreno, like Lewin, wanted to create effective problem-solving groups, but instead of giving more skills to the leader or training the group as a whole, Moreno approached the problem through the individual by surrounding each person with a compatible set of other persons. If an individual had undergone some personal crisis that made it difficult to choose effectively or to replace some loss in the individual's primary social atom (composed of family and intimate friends), then Moreno would recommend "psychodrama" as a method of group therapy. In a psychodrama the "protagonist" acts out scenes involving problems, on a stage, with the help of a therapist-director, and other persons who take the parts of significant persons, objects, or ideas in the drama. Ideally, the protagonist reaches some emotional catharsis freeing that person from old ways of relating to and perceiving others and makes it possible to go on to new insights and new solutions to the old problems.

A third approach to the study of social interaction is represented by the work of Bales at Harvard University, where he has been throughout his academic career. Bales did not promote an application of his theories and for the first ten years of his research on small groups there was almost no applied side. Bales and his colleagues were identified during this period by their use of the category system for *Interaction Process Analysis* (Bales, 1950) and for their laboratory studies of initially leaderless groups of college students. Few, if any, experimental manipulations were used in the laboratory. The observers focused on the process of group problem-solving. As a sociologist, Bales was primarily interested in the study of small groups as a social system, and only started to consider the individual and his personality in the 1960s. During this period, Bales (1970) also shifted from the use of 12 categories for interaction process analysis to the use of three dimensions for the analysis of interpersonal behavior (upward-downward, positive-negative, and forward-backward).

In the late 1950s, Bales took over the direction of a course in the group dynamics tradition that had been developed at the Harvard Business School. The course had been based almost entirely on class discussions of human relations cases, but after it was moved to the Social Relations Department more and more sessions were introduced in which group members would discuss their own group process. Since the course was popular, a number of teaching assistants were needed to lead the groups. Some of these persons in turn reported research on various aspects of the group's activity (Mills, 1964; Dunphy, 1964; Slater, 1966; Mann, Gibbard, and Hartman, 1967). Bales himself had moved out from behind the observer's window to participate as a leader in some of the groups. He now set his goal as developing a set of techniques that could be used by group members as well as observers for the analysis of group process. This led to the production of an elaborate system for the simultaneous multilevel observation of groups (Bales, Cohen, and Williamson, 1979).

The term "sociometry" first appeared as a heading in the index for the *Psychological Abstracts* in 1940 with reference to the work of Moreno and his colleagues. Next the term "group dynamics" was introduced in 1945 with reference to the work of Lewin. In 1950, the term "small group" appeared with reference to Bales's book *Interaction Process Analysis* (1950). The three schools of sociometry, group dynamics, and small groups dominated the field through the 1960s with the group dynamics approach appealing more to psychologists and the small groups approach appealing more to sociologists.

As a result of being associated with Bales, first while I was a postdoctoral student and later as one of his research assistants from 1953 through 1960, my own work has been largely influenced by his approach and the Harvard "functional" theory of Parsons and others. However the differences between the three schools are mainly a matter of emphasis rather than in presenting entirely different sets of ideas. As evidence one can note that the collections of readings on *Group Dynamics* (Cartwright and Zander, 1968) and *Small Groups* (Hare, Borgatta, and Bales, 1965) contain articles from all three schools.

As a final note on the sources of research for the present analysis of social interaction and creativity in small groups, one can observe that psychologists dominate the field, followed by sociologists, and then by persons in the applied fields of psychotherapy, education, social work, and business. In some cases those who are part of the "group dynamics" school are concerned with groups much larger than the typical "small" group of five to twenty members. On the other hand, many of the social-psychologists who have made contributions to the understanding of social interaction in small groups were not studying groups as such but rather individual behavior in a social situation. Thus recent work on cognitive balance (Heider, 1958), bargaining (Deutsch and Krauss, 1960), risk taking (Wallach, Kogan, and Bem, 1962), social exchange (Chadwick-Jones, 1976), helping behavior (Darley and Latané, 1968), competition and cooperation (Pruitt and Kimmel, 1977), or the use of personal space (Evans and Howard, 1973), is all relevant even though the behavior may not have been observed in a small group context. For all the research in this area, relatively few persons work in a general theoretical context that provides a way of integrating the various research results. The best developed and most comprehensive scheme to date is the one provided by Bales and his colleagues (1979).

This introduction has not included an historical account of the main features in the development of the study of creativity since this has been independent, for the most part, of the research on group dynamics. Although a few persons have contributed to research in both areas, I do not have the same degree of familiarity with the work on creativity as I do with the study of social interaction in small groups. The material on creativity that I have included in this volume, mainly in Chapter 10, is drawn primarily from recent collections of papers that were given at symposia on creativity in the United States. From these papers and other volumes I have selected the facts and theories that fit most easily with the four perspectives that I have found helpful for the analysis of group dynamics.

PART I

FOUR PERSPECTIVES ON SOCIAL INTERACTION

The first part of the book introduces four perspectives that can be used in the analysis of interaction in small groups: four functional categories for the analysis of content, four interaction dimensions for the analysis of process, and two perspectives that combine some of these categories. The dramaturgical perspective highlights the extent to which interaction unfolds as a play with a series of acts. The method of exchange analysis is concerned with the commodities, in terms of functional categories, that are given or received in the course of social interaction.

Chapter 1
A Functional Perspective

The functional perspective as it has been developed by Parsons (1961) and others is a comprehensive theory that has been used primarily for the analysis of action in large social systems rather than in small groups. In this chapter we will consider only three parts of this theory. The first hypothesis is that social action can be analyzed at different system levels, the second is that at each level there are four basic problems that must be solved if the system is to survive, and the third is that the concept of the "cybernetic hierarchy of control" can be applied to the analysis of social behavior.

The chapter concludes with an indication of the five decisions that must be made by an observer who wishes to use the functional (AGIL) categories for the analysis of the content of interaction in small groups, and an example of the use of the category system in the observation of a problem-solving group of university students.

System Levels and the Interaction Process

The system levels appearing in most theoretical analyses of social interaction are given in Figure 1.1. There are four major system levels—cultural, social system, personality, and biological—with the most direct effect on social interaction, plus a fifth area of the surrounding environment that includes the natural and man-made nonhuman setting in which the interaction occurs.

A person's *biological nature* and the *environment* represent a different order of data than the other levels since they can be measured independently of the social behavior that one wishes to predict. However the *personality* of the individual and the nature of the *social system* and *culture* are all abstractions from social behavior. Those tendencies in an

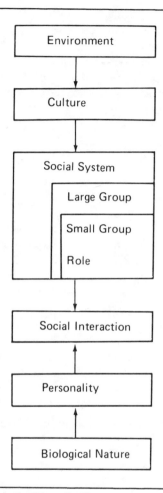

Figure 1.1 System Levels in the Interaction Process

individual's behavior that are consistent as the individual moves from group to group are called *personality*. The expectations shared by group members about the behavior associated with some position in a small or large group, no matter who fills the position, are called *role*. Sets of roles make up the *social system*. The *culture* of the society provides the set of values that gives meaning to life and death as well as guidance in human affairs. It includes the patterns of behavior that are transmitted from one generation to the next: ways of thinking, acting, and feeling.

To predict some aspects of social interaction we need know only how an individual's biological nature typically responds to the environment.

For some predictions, particularly in psychiatric settings, personality may be the dominant variable. However, we can predict many details of everyday life if we know only the roles played in the groups to which a person belongs. In general we would find that an individual's behavior is some compromise between the tendencies of personality and the expectations of role. Four basic dimensions that can be used to describe personality, interaction, and role are given in Chapter 2.

The Small Group

There is no definite cutting point in the continuum between a collection of individuals, such as one might find waiting for a bus on a corner, and a fully organized group. There is also no definite cutting point between the small, intimate, face-to-face group and the large, formal group. For a collection of individuals to be considered a group, there must be some interaction and some evidence that the four basic functional needs of groups are being met. The group must have a set of *values* to give meaning to its activity, a set of *norms* that specify the role relationships between the members, some form of *leadership* to carry out specific tasks, and some means of providing *resources* that are needed to reach the group's goal.

Small groups include those having from two up to about twenty members. However, even larger groups may be considered "small" if face-to-face interaction is possible. Also, collections of fewer than twenty persons may contain several subgroups. The most commonly used definition of a small group has been that given by Bales (1950: 33):

> A small group is defined as any number of persons engaged in interaction with each other in a single face-to-face meeting or a series of meetings, in which each member receives some impression or perception of each other member distinct enough so that he can, either at the time or in later questioning, give some reaction to each of the others as an individual person, even though it be only to recall that the other person was present.

Form, Process, and Content of Interaction

Social interaction has three aspects: form, process, and content (see Figure 1.2). The two variables involved in the *form* of interaction are more easily recorded than either the process or the content. As one approaches a group from the outside, the first aspect of interaction that becomes

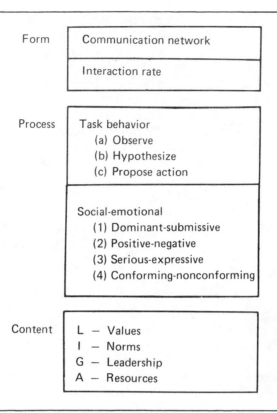

Figure 1.2 Paradigm for the Analysis of Interaction

apparent is the communication network (who speaks to whom), and next the amount of interaction carried by each of the communication channels.[1]

For a closer analysis of the group, one needs some *process* categories and some *content* categories. With a few exceptions, such as the system devised by Carr (1929), most of the category systems developed for the observation of individual or group behavior have been concerned with *process*. The most widely used of these systems was the one proposed by Bales (1950) composed of 12 categories such as "Shows solidarity," "Shows agreement," "Gives opinion," and "Asks for suggestion." For most observers this was enough since they were studying groups of a particular kind (that is, students solving human relations problems or patients in group therapy) where the general content of the problem could be described in a few words.

Among the *process* category systems the most frequent division is between process directed primarily toward the solution of task problems and process directed primarily toward the solution of social-emotional problems. Many category systems, such as those of Bales (1950) and Bion (1961), include both types of process, while some concentrate only in one area. Within the task area the minimum set of categories would parallel the steps in the scientific method, namely observation, hypothesis formation, and the testing of hypotheses.[2] Within the social-emotional area the four process dimensions that are described in Chapter 2 are the most prominent, namely: dominant-submissive, positive-negative, serious-expressive, and conforming-nonconforming.

For the analysis of the *content* of the task, a set of four categories representing the four functional problems of groups (values, norms, leadership, and resources) provides some basic differentiations. This set can easily be expanded to 16 by considering the same four categories as subtasks within each functional area. The definitions of these categories are given later in this chapter and examples of their use appear throughout the text.

Four Functional Categories

Up to this point several references have been made to the four functional categories without being very explicit about the contents of the categories or their relations to each other. The following section includes operational definitions for the categories as they have been used for the analysis of behavior in small groups. This is only one application of a comprehensive theory developed by Parsons and his colleagues for the analysis of social systems (Parsons, 1961; Effrat, 1968; Loubser et al., 1976). A reader already familiar with functional theory from other sources should note that the definitions of the *adaptive* (A) and *goal-attainment* (G) sectors as they are used here differ in certain respects from Parsons's formulations. The present set of categories was proposed by Effrat especially for analysis of small groups.

The fundamental idea in functional theory is that all groups, whether small discussion groups or whole societies, if they are to survive, must meet four basic needs: (L) the member must share some common identity and have some commitment to the values of the group, (A) they must have or be able to generate the skills and resources necessary to reach the group goal, (I) they must have rules that allow them to coordinate their activity and enough feeling of solidarity to stay together to complete the task, and finally (G) they must be able to exercise enough control over their membership to be effective in reaching their common goal.

The formal names of the AGIL categories are: Adaptation, Goal-attainment, Integration, and Latent pattern maintenance and tension management (or simply pattern maintenance). These same terms, or more frequently their first letters, A,G,I, and L, will be used throughout the text. The term "adaptation" does not precisely fit the present definition of this category. In Parsons's description of a social system the "adaptive" area was the area in which the system related or "adapted" to the outside environment or to other systems. In the present definition the emphasis is on the production of resources for internal use.

The relatively long title of the "L" sector of "Latent pattern maintenance and tension management" has several ideas packed into it. The central idea is that every group needs a set of values and that a pattern of activity must be maintained in line with these values if the group is to have integrity. The term "latent" appears because members of most groups only have face-to-face meetings on occasion. During this period the group is "manifest." However during the periods between meetings the group is "latent." Thus, the process of pattern maintenance must be strong enough not only to set general guidelines for the group while the members are present but also to provide enough commitment so that the members will return for the next meeting. The idea of "tension management" is included in the title because too much tension, especially that associated with the success or failure of work in the "G" area, can dissolve the group if the tension is not managed. In general, any activity that has to do with the initial selection of members for the group, their initiation into the rights and duties of membership, and their commitment to the group activity falls in the "L" area.

In a large social system, such as a nation, the four categories (AGIL) are represented by the economic, political, legal, and familial and religious substructures. For each of these substructures there is a generalized medium of exchange (money, power, influence, and commitments), a value principle that guides the action in this area (utility, effectiveness, solidarity, and integrity), and a standard of coordination for activity (solvency, success, consensus, and pattern consistency). A summary of these concepts is given in Figure 1.3.

Thus, an activity that seems to be primarily *economic*, such as raising money to be used for the general purposes of the group, where the focus is on utility with a concern for solvency, would be classified in the A or *Adaptive* sector. In contrast, an activity that seemed religious or familial, that had to do with forming basic commitments to the group, was concerned with its integrity, and related to the consistency of its pattern of activity over time would be classified in the L or *Pattern maintenence* sector. In a similar way the other activities of a group would be classified

A   G

(1) Adaptation	(1) Goal attainment
(2) Economic	(2) Political
(3) Money	(3) Power
(4) Utility	(4) Effectiveness
(5) Solvency	(5) Success
(1) Pattern maintenance	(1) Integration
(2) Familial and Religious	(2) Legal
(3) Commitments	(3) Influence
(4) Integrity	(4) Solidarity
(5) Pattern consistency	(5) Consensus

L   I

Figure 1.3 Substructures, Generalized Media of Exchange, Value Principles, and Standards of Coordination for Four Functional Problems

SOURCE: A. Paul Hare, "Group Decision by Consensus," *Sociological Inquiry* 43 (1973). Reprinted by permission of the editor for Alpha Kappa Delta.

Key: (1) the functional problem
      (2) the substructure at the social system level
      (3) the generalized medium of exchange
      (4) the value principle
      (5) the coordinative standard

as related to the other two functions, *Integration* or *Goal-attainment*. The content of each sector as it would appear in a small group is given in Table 1.1 in the set of functional categories for small group analysis.

The Cybernetic Hierarchy of Control

The "cybernetic hierarchy of control" is a concept that was first used in the analysis of physical systems but it can also be applied to social systems. The basic idea is that a part of a system containing *information* will be able to control a part of a system containing *energy*. The classic everyday example is that of the rider with ideas about where to go (information) being able to control the direction of the horse (energy). In physical systems the thermostat that processes information about temperature is able to control the furnace that produces the heat or a computer is able to control the activity on an industrial production line (Effrat, 1976: 666-669).

In the case of groups, the highly generalized normative elements of the system guide and control the more specific elements of action. Thus, within the total action system, represented in Figure 1.1, the four system levels (cultural, social, personality, and biological) are related to each other

TABLE 1.1   Functional Categories for Small Group Analysis

L Phase + Seeks or provides basic categories or ultimate values
  Asks for or seeks to define:
    basic purpose or identity of group
    fundamental meaning of "all this"
    general orientation
    basic obligations
  − Seeks to deny, take away, or inhibit the development and recognition of values.

I Phase + Seeks or provides solidarity or norms (as primary mechanism of conflict management)
  Asks for or seeks to define:
    how the group can get along better, promote harmony, or decrease conflict.
    what the specific norms governing relations should be
  − Seeks to deny, inhibit, or prevent the formation of norms and movement toward group solidarity

G Phase + Seeks or provides relatively specific direction, goal-definition, or problem solutions relevant to the group's goals.
  Asks for or seeks to define:
    relatively specific group goals (be careful to distinguish from values and norms)
    decisions which in effect are attainment of group's goals
  − Seeks to prevent or inhibit movement toward the group's goals

A Phase + Seeks or provides facilities for goal attainment
  Asks for or seeks to define:
    how to get or increase (especially to generalize) **resources, relevant** information, or facts
  − Seeks to deny, inhibit, or prevent the provision of facilities and relevant information

SOURCE: A. Paul Hare, "Group Decision by Consensus," *Sociological Inquiry* 43 (1973). Reprinted by permission of the editor for Alpha Kappa Delta.

in a cybernetic hierarchy of control. The values represented by the culture are more controlling than the norms of the social system. The norms of the social system are in turn more controlling than the personality of the individual. Finally, the personality characteristics play a more controlling part in social interaction than the biological traits and processes of the physical organism.

Within the social system (or any of the other system levels) the four functional areas, as indicated in Table 1.1, are controlling in the same order. The area of pattern maintenance (L) controls the integrative area

(I), which in turn provides more control than the goal-attainment area (G). The adaptive area (A) ranks lowest in its influence on other parts of the system. One example of the application of the concept of the cybernetic hierarchy in the analysis of small groups is given in Chapter 6 on social control, where the various pressures toward conformity can be seen to be operating in this way.

Coding Social Interaction with the AGIL Categories

In common with other category systems there are five decisions that must be made by anyone using the AGIL category system (Hare, 1976b: 398-399):

(1) *Frame of reference:* Behavior may be scored primarily by the intent of the actor or by its effect on others. Generally, unless one wishes to focus on the difference between intention and effect, the behavior is scored as it would be seen by the average member of the group being observed if the average member was also familiar with AGIL coding. One can also focus on the individual who makes the statement or consider that each statement is a reflection of the group atmosphere at the time and not summarize the data by individuals. In some cases (for example, coding the minutes of meetings), it may only be possible to note that the particular content occurred and not who actually made the statement (Hare, 1968).

(2) *Unit act:* The amount of interaction that takes place before a unit of behavior is scored can be small or large. It can be as small as any bit of behavior to which another person can respond, or a sentence, paragraph, or whole speech or utterance. On the other hand scores might be given only after each "natural" period of a meeting, or after each meeting in a series of meetings. Generally the units used in scoring *content* are larger than those used in scoring *process* since it requires more information to assess the relationship of an action to the functional needs of a group than it does to assess the process involved; for example, whether a person is being positive or negative.

(3) *Sample:* Some observers score continuously and some take short "time samples" at frequent intervals. Bales (1950), who has probably had the most experience using category systems, recommended continuous scoring with his early category system. More recently, he has decided to focus primarily on those actions that have special meaning for the group, including those that contain images (Bales, Cohen, and Williamson, 1979). This is probably what happens in any event if we do not use a conscious sampling method.

(4) *Single or multiple code:* If a given unit of behavior appears to have more than one implication (for example, it may contain both work and

emotion), some observers score the dominant characteristic of the act while others give several scores. In the case of the AGIL categories, one score will usually be given for content although another set of scores (to be described in Chapter 2) may be given for process. However if one wishes to code the functional implications of phases within a given content area (for example L_l, L_a, L_i, and L_g, as in the analysis of group development in Chapter 5) or of phases at different system levels (for example, small group, institution, and social system, as was done by Hare [1968] in the study of a Regional Development Board in the Philippines), then a multiple AGIL code will be used.

(5) *Recording devices:* The observer may rely on memory, make notes, use prepared forms or special recording devices (such as those developed by Bales and Gerbrands [1948] or Chapple [1940; Matarazzo, Saslow, and Matarazzo, 1956]), or make a record by tape recorder, television, or movie camera that can be used later for coding. If the activity is not coded directly, while it happens, it usually takes considerable time to recover the information, especially if written protocols are transcribed from some recording device. In addition, some aspects of interaction may be lost if only voice is recorded or if the television or movie camera is kept at a fixed angle. However audio-visual recordings have an advantage in that they can be played over and over again to check self-self and interobserver reliability in the use of the category system.

The example that follows shows the use of the AGIL system in the analysis of a problem-solving group of students at Kent State University in 1970 during the period of student protest in the United States. I was a participant observer, using some notes, but relying primarily on memory for the analysis since the intrusion of direct recording devices would have been inappropriate (Hare, 1972: 365-367).

Some Observations at Kent State University: Or, Who Needs a Revolution to be a Human Being?

It was Thursday night, October 1, 1970, at Kent State University. "Think Week" was going well so far. For the past several years, the first week of classes had been designated by the student government as "Think Week." During this period outside speakers were brought on campus for a series of lectures and discussions on current topics. This year Kent had plenty to think about following the events of the previous May when four students were killed and others wounded by members of the national guard. This year the subject of discussion was nonviolence and its application to Kent State in the form of life style, avoiding further violence, and creative dissent. The theme was "Power to the Peaceful."

The week before, many of the students, faculty, and administration were fearful that the University would not be able to last through the first week. Someone might place a bomb in a building, the president of the university might be attacked while giving his opening speech to students, dissident students who were rumored to have transferred to the campus in large numbers might start a riot. Between 30 and 40 rumors were actively circulating about the campus, and all of them boded no good.

However, from Monday to Thursday there had been no major problems. The president had spoken at the opening convocation without incident. The memorial service Monday night—with songs by Phil Ochs, and stirring speeches by Ralph Abernathy, recalling the power of nonviolence in the days of Martin Luther King, and Ira Sandperl, representing the California "life style" approach—roused the audience of about 7,000 to the possibilities of nonviolent action. The candlelight march from the gym to the common where the students had been shot closed an emotional evening.

On Tuesday, Wednesday, and Thursday there was an almost continuous stream of nonviolent activity flowing across the campus. Representatives from "Nader's Raiders," the Berkeley Peace Brigade, and the "Harvard Peace Action" conducted workshops on nonviolent life styles and forms of protest. James Michener, Mark Lane, and Congressman Robert Eckhart gave major addresses in the evening, and journalists, legislators, and attorneys spoke about problems of civil liberties and the democratic system. Friday was to bring more workshops, speeches by Allard Lowenstein, Democratic congressman from New York, and Sargent Shriver, former Peace Corps director. The final event was to be an informal celebration of Gandhi's 101st birthday featuring a film of Gandhi's life and discussions of new directions for those who had been moved to join some form of nonviolent activity.

Since the number of students attending the various speeches and workshops had ranged from about 30 to about 300, the number of students who would participate in the final event was not expected to be high. By my count, about 40 were actually present the next night, not including the outside resource people and the 20 or so students who were committed to nonviolence before Think Week began. This is a very small percentage of a student body of 20,000. However, it would increase the number of activists about three-fold, giving more than enough problems to the "old timers" as they sought to *integrate* the activities of all these new *individuals* into the "movement."

The emphasis was clearly on the word "integrate" since the word "organize" was ruled out as a "no-no." The problem that the "old timers" had set for themselves was to help the newcomers find their places in the nonviolent life without "organizing" them and without clear directions from any appointed or self-appointed leaders. The problem was to bring about change in old forms of social institutions, including Kent State University, using a seemingly new form of group process which allowed much more freedom to the individual but at the same time called on the individual for more commitment and responsibility in his actions and more concern for his fellows. The goal was to become more "humane" and to treat others in more humanizing ways rather than to dehumanize them in large formal institutions or, in the extreme case, to treat them as objects for target practice in a shooting gallery. For some, old and young, who felt comfortable with clearly designated leaders, agenda, and formal controls, this new life style seemed strange, ineffective, even revolutionary. Why should it seem so revolutionary? Who needs a revolution to be a human being? To discover something of the nature of this "revolution" let us return to the events of Thursday night at Kent State to watch the process unfold.

Problem-Solving

The first students arrived at the apartment about 10:30 p.m., after the evening speaker. Over the next hour about eight students assembled, some first passing by the kitchen for snacks, others lying on a large mattress in the corner of the room where they rested, attempting to recover from the fatigue of the many preceding nights of planning and "organizing" with little sleep. The apartment was one of several rented by members of an informal "commune" of students who shared each others' food and facilities and were always open to any visitors from the movement who might want to stay overnight.

As students joined the group they would volunteer information about their activities during the day, or they might be drawn out by another group member. There was no appointed leader for the group and no agenda. The center of the discussion would shift from one person to another as the topic changed. In general, the person with the most information on a particular subject became the "leader" of the discussion while that subject held the floor. Early in the evening one member reported his conversation with some students who planned to burn their draft cards. He had suggested they say that they were inspired by the president of the university, who had made a public statement endorsing nonviolence. Other group members challenged this stand, arguing that one should not single out an individual for attack in a nonviolent campaign. Variations on the theme were suggested as the group sought to assess the proposed action in the light of Gandhi's search for truth.

Later in the evening the phone rang. A member of the nonviolent action group was calling in from another part of the campus to report yelling in front of one of the dorms. One member of the group took the initiative to go off to check out the report. On his return he reported that it was only a "panty raid" conducted by some male undergraduates at one of the women's dorms. The campus police were on hand and there seemed to be no need for student marshals. Since all members of the group had been trained to act as "third party" marshals in the event of any campus disorder, there was some anxious discussion while the report of the yelling was being checked. The previous events leading to the shooting had taken place over a weekend from May 1 to 4. This was now October 1 and a weekend was approaching. Would this be some sort of "anniversary" of the first event? Would this be the long-feared riot which would provide an occasion for outside authorities to close the university? If so, what could be done to keep it open? Fortunately the group never had to give a final answer to these questions that night, but they realized that plans had to be made for each contingency and that they had no clear plans at present.

As the evening wore on into the early hours of the morning, the group moved back and forth between a number of topics. Plans were developed for a proposed Life Center, schedules were considered for further training of marshals, coordination with other colleges was discussed, and a list was drawn up of current issues which might be the focus of student protest. One woman spoke of her plans for a new course on nonviolence to be given as part of the "free university." Group members considered their own need for more organizing experience. To meet this need and to provide some respite from the stress of opening week, group members planned a weekend workshop with a local resource person at a site some distance from the campus.

Content of Interaction

By the time the evening was over, the group had dealt with three levels of organization: their own group, their group as part of a Life Center, and the Life Center as part of Kent State University. At each level they had discussed aspects of the four basic problems of all social systems: pattern maintenance, adaptation, integration, and goal-attainment. For example, for their own group they discussed their basic values of nonviolence and also the ways in which they would introduce new members to these values (Pattern Maintenance); they considered new sources of information and skills for problem-solving (Adaptation); they shared in the fellowship of food and drink—potato chips and soft drinks—(Integration); and they actually carried out their responsibility as third party marshals by checking out the potential riot (Goal-attainment).

In planning for the Life Center they considered its basic purposes (L); the amount of money, floor space, and office supplies that would be needed (A); the type of committee structure and leadership necessary (I); and the type of programs it would sponsor (G). Similarly, they considered the ways that the Center would fit into the activities of the university.

Thus this form of "leaderless group discussion" was handling a complicated set of problems which the group faced. It was able to do it without the heavy authoritarian structure which the nonviolent movement seeks to replace. The means were consistent with the ends. However, this probably represented the group working at its best. Would the group always be able to perform this way? Would other groups composed in different ways be as successful? Some of these same students were reported on another occasion to have taken 15 or 20 minutes to decide which restaurant to choose for dinner. Why was there a difference?

The literature on role differentiation in groups suggests that when there is a clear basis for role differentiation, group members can more easily recognize informal leaders and spend more time on the task and less time on interpersonal relationships. Perhaps on the evening of October 1 there was a fairly clear differentiation of skills and information for the different topics of discussion. Thus different members would be able to "take over" the "leadership" as the group moved from topic to topic. This would maintain an overall equality of participation and yet reward members for visible abilities. In contrast, the task of choosing a restaurant was probably more one of personal opinion. If no one had any obvious basis for taking the lead, then one person's suggestion could only be followed at the expense of having another's "put down." This would seem an assertion of undue authority to people who are very sensitive about the subject.

Summary

Three parts of the functional perspective developed by Parsons are adapted for use in the analysis of social interaction in small groups. The first is the existence of four major system levels to be considered: cultural, social system, personality, and biological. In addition to these system levels, the surrounding physical environment is also important. The second is that at each system level there are four basic problems that must be solved if the system is to survive. In the small group the solutions to these problems are represented by the values (L) that give meaning to its activity, the norms (I) that specify role relationships between members, the leadership (G) that provides the control of the work of the group, and the resources (A) that are necessary to do the work. The third is that the four system levels as well as the four functional areas are related to each other in a "cybernetic hierarchy" in the order L,I,G, and A, with L being the most controlling and A the least.

A small group may contain from two to more than twenty members. A group is *small* if the members can meet face-to-face. A set of individuals is a *group* if in their interaction they give some evidence of meeting the four basic needs.

For the analysis of social interaction, one can distinguish two aspects of *form,* the communication network and the amount of interaction carried by each channel in the network. The verbal and nonverbal behavior in the group also has two aspects, *process* and *content.* Although many different types of process categories have been proposed, they generally include some *task* or problem-solving categories and some *social-emotional* categories. The content of a discussion may also be categorized in different ways. One comprehensive way is to use the four functional (AGIL) categories. Operational definitions have been provided for each category by Effrat.

To use any category system there are five decisions to be made by the observer: frame of reference, unit act, sample, single or multiple code, and recording device.

In an example of the use of the AGIL content categories, a "leaderless" group of Kent State University students was described as it solved a series of problems at the height of the period of student protest in the United States.

Notes

1. The frequency of interaction is sometimes represented by the number of contributions, sometimes by the relationship between the number and duration of contributions (that is, action and silence), and sometimes by the number of contributions times the average duration of each (that is, total talking time).

2. If we wished to focus on creativity, as we will in Chapter 10, then in the task area we would recognize four levels of creativity: technical, inventive, innovative, and emergentive (Taylor, 1975).

Chapter 2

Four Dimensions
of Interaction

Some of the earliest category systems were developed in the 1920s for the observation of the behavior of children. Usually these systems took the form of a list of behaviors that were presumed to be independent. However, most of the lists were so long that many of the behaviors occurred only infrequently and were not useful in analysis. In addition, it became evident that many of the "independent" behaviors were in fact correlated. With the advent of the statistical procedure for factor analysis used to find underlying dimensions of intelligence and the high speed computer with a memory, it was possible to analyze large sets of data to search for the underlying dimensions of personality and of interpersonal behavior. Although some investigators were concerned only with personality and others with interpersonal behavior, in many cases the same research team was involved. Only a brief summary of the main contributions to this search is given here, with the emphasis on the work of Chapple (1940), Leary (1957), Couch (1960), and Bales (1970, 1979).

Chapple's One-Dimensional Approach

Chapple (1940) had a theory that the most important characteristic of an individual's interaction was total amount of talking. He usually observed two persons at one time, in an interview situation, recording the frequency and duration of their speeches and silences on a machine that he called the Interaction Chronograph. Although he generated a number of indices from various combinations of his chronograph measures, a factor analysis indicated that there was still only one basic dimension being measured, namely action-silence (Matarazzo, Saslow, and Hare, 1958).

Bales and other investigators were convinced that life was more compli-cated than this and continued to look for additional dimensions, however action and silence (or dominance and submission) has turned out to be the first factor in all subsequent systems. Part of the reason for this is that total interaction is an important characteristic, part of the reason is that the process and content of interaction is determined so much by the requirements of the task in any given situation that once you know the amount of interaction a person is initiating, you can easily predict the other characteristics of the pattern on the other dimensions. That is, in most situations there is such a high correlation between the different dimensions of behavior that it is difficult to provide evidence for more than one factor. The observations of several observers seem to be more reliable for this factor and less reliable for the others.

Leary's Interpersonal Diagnosis of Personality

Leary and his colleagues working at the Kaiser Clinic in California supplied evidence for the second dimension presented in the book *Inter-personal Dimensions of Personality* (1957). This was based primarily on their experience as clinical psychologists, both in providing psychological counseling and therapy and in developing psychological tests. Leary showed how 16 psychological types of interpersonal behavior could be arranged in a circle and described in turn as combinations of two principal axes: dominance-submission (vertical axis) and positive-negative, or love-hate (horizontal axis reading from right to left). Leary suggested that personality was an interpersonal phenomenon and that actions on the part of one person would tend to "pull" actions on the part of another. For example, dominant behavior would tend to "pull" submissive behavior, and vice versa, whereas positive behavior would pull positive and negative would pull negative. Combinations of these behaviors would pull the expected combination in return. Thus, bitter rebellious behavior (negative and submissive) would pull punitive rejection and superiority from others.

Couch's Psychological Determinants of Interpersonal Behavior

Couch's doctoral dissertation at Harvard University on "Psychological Determinants of Interpersonal Behavior" (1960) is the most relevant work for the present analysis. His study is based on observations of 12 groups of five undergraduates each, working on a variety of tasks over five meetings. (Bales and Kassebaum assisted with the observations.) As part of the laboratory experiment, each subject was given a long battery of psychological tests and some of the subjects were interviewed in depth. The dissertation includes a series of factor analyses of different domains of interpersonal behavior: overt behavior, perception, personality characteristics, concealment defenses, apperceptions, and behavior received.

As a final tour de force, Couch performed a factor analysis of 300 variables drawn from all of the domains he had investigated. Altogether about 600 variables had been involved in the various factor analyses. He abstracted six factors that accounted for most of the variance:

(1) Interpersonal dominance (dominant vs. submissive)
(2) Interpersonal affect (positive vs. negative)
(3) Social expressivity (expressive vs. serious)
(4) Influence attempts
(5) Surface acquiescence
(6) Conventional behavior (conforming vs. nonconforming)

The first factor accounted for about twice as much of the variance as the second factor, and about four times as much as the other four factors.

Bales's Three Dimensions of Social Evaluation

After Couch had demonstrated the possibility of adding more factors to Leary's set of two, Bales shifted from the use of 12 separate categories (1950), that had stood him and others in such good stead for so many years, to the use of a *dimensional* approach. He also changed his position for observation. He was no longer a hidden observer behind a one-way mirror but now took his place in the classroom as the trainer in a "self-analytic" group. His primary concern was no longer to provide a set of categories for professional scientists to use in their laboratory studies of groups, but to provide group members with a way of evaluating their own behavior and that of the other group members.

Using Couch's thesis as a source of primary data Bales (1970) first presented a detailed scheme of 26 types of interpersonal behavior where the types represented combinations of three dimensions. In his next work with Cohen and Williamson (1979), Bales showed how this approach could be used to code simultaneously several levels of interaction with a focus on the "images" that guide group action. The three dimensions are the first two of Couch (and Leary) plus a fusion of a reversal of Couch's third dimension and his sixth dimension. Bales called his dimensions:

(1) Upward-downward (dominant vs. submissive)

(2) Positive-negative
(3) Forward-backward (serious and conforming vs. expressive and nonconforming)

Bales stopped at three dimensions for much the same reason as Chapple stopped at one and Leary at two. Given the measures he had and the behavior he wished to predict, he seemed to have accounted for as much of the variance as he could. Three dimensions have a further advantage in that they can be visualized in relation to the three-dimensional physical space in which the subject moves.

The Fourth Dimension

I would have been quite happy to go along with Bales's three dimensions and Parson's four functions had it not been for the research on nonviolent action mentioned in the introduction. Given the desirability of combining Parsons's functional categories for content with Bales's dimensions for process I tried, unsuccessfully, to combine four with three. It appeared that the work would be simpler if there were actually four categories in each set. Recalling that Bales had actually fused two of Couch's factors, it did not require a great deal of ingenuity to reread Couch's thesis to see if the factors as they were originally described might provide a solution. The separation of Bales's third factor into two leaves the third factor as "serious vs. expressive." The fourth factor becomes "conforming vs nonconforming," thus giving emphasis to an aspect of interaction that has been a concern of social-psychologists since the earliest recorded research. In Couch's thesis the most stable reference point for the new fourth factor was the observers rating or group members on "authoritarian values," and is thus related to the "F" (authoritarianism) Scale that has been used in so much of the research on conformity.

The fourth factor of conforming-nonconforming has some of the characteristics of *time,* the fourth factor in physical space. In the physical world, *time* is related to *change.* In the long run, during the time that it takes light to reach the earth from a distant star, the light can be bent (changed in its direction) by its interaction with passing planets. However in the short run, say in the time it takes light to travel from one place to another on earth, time need not be considered. The three dimensions of height, length, and width are sufficient for locating the position of objects on the earth. In a similar way, in the short run, the three dimensions of upward-downward, positive-negative, and forward-backward are enough to locate behaviors or roles or images in social space. However in the long run it is helpful to note those individuals who indicate their concern for maintaining the status quo (the conformers) and those who indicate their resistance to the present system or their desire to change it (the nonconformers; see Chapter 8 on roles).

In 1953, Parsons and Bales had indicated the probable relationship between Bales's earlier 12-category system and Parsons's four functions, but they never actually tried out the two schemes simultaneously on the same group (Parsons, Bales, and Shils, 1953). Thus, not only could one expect the two systems to be related but also the present version of the AGIL categories, given in Chapter 1, was constructed with the Bales categories in mind. The expected relationship between the two sets of categories is as follows:

	Functional Content Categories		*Interaction Process Dimensions*
L —	Pattern maintenence	IV.	Conforming vs nonconforming
I —	Integration	II.	Positive vs negative
G —	Goal attainment	I.	Dominant vs submissive
A —	Adaptation	III.	Serious vs expressive

Thus when the group is working on a problem of pattern maintenance we would expect the dimension of "conforming vs. nonconforming" behavior to be the most salient, although behavior on the other three dimensions would also be in evidence. In a similar way we would expect positive and negative behavior to be most visible when the group is working on a problem of integration, dominant and submissive behavior when problems of goal attainment involve leadership and organization for the task, and serious and expressive behavior when the focus in the group is on the production of resources or learning new skills. These relationships have been illustrated by a double coding of chapters from the novel *Lord of the Flies* (Hare, 1978a) and by observations in a role-playing experiment that is described in Chapter 6 (Hare, Kritzer, and Blumberg, 1979).

Operational definitions of the four dimensions are given in two forms, first as they would be used to distinguish only the two ends of each dimension (Table 2.1) and next as they would be used to distinguish seven points along each of the dimensions (Table 2.2).

As an example of the use of the four dimensions as they are defined in Table 2.1, the following brief accounts describe the interaction between two nonviolent protesters and representatives of the U.S. Government (Hare, 1972: 363-365).

TABLE 2.1   Interaction Process Analysis, Four Dimensions

I Dominant vs Submissive

Dominant:	Assuming autocratic control or seeking status in the group by making direct suggestions or by giving opinions which serve to guide group activity. (Also measured by total talking rate.)
Submissive:	Showing dependence by asking for help, showing anxiety, shame and guilt, or frustration, laughing at the jokes of a dominant person.

II Positive vs Negative

Positive:	Seeming friendly by showing affection, agreement, or by asking for information or opinion in an encouraging way.
Negative:	Seeming unfriendly by disagreeing, showing antagonism, or diffuse aggression.

III Serious vs Expressive

Serious:	Giving information or opinions which indicate serious involvement in the task. Routine agreement.
Expressive:	Giving support to others regardless of task performance or showing tension release through joking or other evidence of flight from the task.

IV Conforming vs. Nonconforming

Conforming:	Seeking to be guided by the group norms by asking for information or suggestions. Making jokes or dramatic statements which reveal the basic nature of the group.
Nonconforming:	Showing tension which indicates withdrawal from the field. Describing fantasies which reveal individual goals rather than group goals. Resisting pressure to conform.

SOURCE: A. Paul Hare, "Four Dimensions of Interpersonal Behavior," *Psychological Reports* 30 (1972): 499-512. Reprinted by permission of the publisher.

A Demonstration Against War Taxes

On April 15, 1970, members of our research team were on hand at the internal revenue headquarters in Philadelphia to observe a demonstration conducted by the Philadelphia War Tax Resisters group. During the early hours of the morning there were as many observers on the street as demonstrators. We sought to test the reliability of our four-dimensional category system for rating inter-action process. Several observers would watch the demonstrator for about five minutes and then make a summary rating on each of the four dimensions. In this

TABLE 2.2   Four Dimensions: Observer's Recording Sheet

	Subject Rating
I. *Dominant-Submissive*	
Very dominant – more dominant than necessary, pushing, not allowing others to speak, shouting.	_____7
Dominant – continually initiating conversation, blocking path.	_____6
Slightly dominant – any slight hint of dominance, approaching the other person, occasionally initiating dialogue.	_____5
Neutral	_____4
Slightly submissive – the slightest bit submissive, hesitating, avoiding looking at the other person.	_____3
Submissive – backing off, obviously avoiding the other person, speaking only when spoken to, acknowledging an order.	_____2
Very submissive – running away, cringing.	_____1
II. *Positive-Negative*	
Very positive – "gushing," hugging, kissing, other signs of extreme affection.	_____7
Positive – agreeing, smiling, encouraging, overt signs of friendliness.	_____6
Slightly positive – the slightest signs of friendliness, smiling, being pleasant.	_____5
Neutral	_____4
Slightly negative – not smiling, gloomy.	_____3
Negative – hostile, challenging, disagreeing.	_____2
Very negative – nasty, angry.	_____1
III. *Serious-Expressive*	
Very serious – soberly involved in task with indications of high inertia, i.e., would be difficult to move to a lighter vein. Indications of anxiety about turning from task.	_____7
Serious – giving information or opinions that indicate serious involvement in the task.	_____6
Slightly serious – routine agreement or other indications that individual is paying attention to the work.	_____5
Neutral	_____4
Slightly expressive – smiling or other indications that individual finds situation amusing and is not very involved.	_____3
Expressive – joking and laughing or other forms of relief from the tension of the serious nature of the task.	_____2
Very expressive – giving support to others regardless of task performance. Obvious signs of flight from the task (through fantasy or acting out) that make it difficult for others to do serious work.	_____1
IV. *Conforming-Nonconforming*	
Very conforming – Clear statements or action indicating that others should stay in line with group norms.	_____7
Conforming – seeking to be guided by group norms by asking for information or suggestions. Revealing a constriction of fantasy life and social patterns in line with group norms.	_____6

(continued on p. 40)

TABLE 2.2   Continued

	Subject Rating
Slightly conforming – acting in an accepted way for this group, especially in response to requests for conformity.	_____ 5
Neutral	_____ 4
Slightly nonconforming – shows tension or slight resistance to group activity.	_____ 3
Nonconforming – acting in ways that are clearly different from majority, although within accepted limits for the group as a whole.	_____ 2
Very nonconforming – withdrawing from the field, describing fantasies that reveal individual goals rather than group goals. Urging anarchistic values.	_____ 1

case, we had previously observed the demonstrators in the course of weekend workshops and had obtained personality and background information from them. Two short sequences of interaction will illustrate the use of the category system.

The first demonstrator, a man of about 60 years whom we will call Bill, had been walking back and forth in front of the main entrance of the internal revenue headquarters. He carried a sign which read " Don't pay war taxes." In general he seemed serious and intent on his work but would smile when a pedestrian stopped to talk to him. It was a cold, windy day. After a few hours of picketing, Bill decided to go inside the building to visit the toilet. He was stopped at the door by two men, and the conversation went something like this:

Man: Where are you going?
Bill: I don't have to tell you where I'm going.
Man: (showing his U.S. marshal badge): Why do you want to come in here?
Bill: Just because you have a badge doesn't mean I have to tell you anything.
Man: You still can't come in here.

At this point Bill left the entrance and solved his problem elsewhere.

Although Bill had been dominant and positive with passing pedestrians, he was clearly negative with the U.S. marshals. In both cases he was serious, but with the marshals he was definitely nonconforming since he refused to go along with their definition of the situation. Here we see a marked difference in Bill's behavior toward the pedestrian whom he would like to influence and the marshal whom he makes no attempt to reach. This may provide a partial answer to the initial research question concerning the origins of the violence in nonviolent demonstrations. It is possible that demonstrators are not uniformly loving and concerned about all persons present at a demonstration. It is also possible that when authority figures "come on strong" as they did in this instance, it is difficult for a demonstrator not to respond defensively without very specific training in his role.

A second incident occurred at the same demonstration. The demonstrator of college age, whom we will call Fred, entered the foyer of the internal revenue headquarters with his income tax form. He had hoped to make some verbal protest while handing in his form at the office inside. The following conversation was recorded on a tape recorder he was carrying.

Agent: Can I help you, buddy?

Fred: I have a tax form. I want to give it to someone inside.

Agent: (asking to see the form): Are you going to file it? Do you want to mail it?

Fred: No. I want to give it to them.

Agent: Do you want to file it?

1st Agent: Put it in the basket over there.

2nd Agent: I'll take it. I suggest you sign it. (The agent has noticed that Fred has not yet signed his form.)

Fred: Oh, yeah.

Agent: W-2 form attached?

Fred: I can't go into the office?

Agent: No!

Fred: Why is that?

Agent: We are using the place over here to collect returns. There is a mailbox over here. Right here.

Fred: I want to go into the office to give it to them.

Agent: Drop it here, this is it. This is the mail drop right here. This takes care of it. Have you got a pen? (To sign the form.)

Fred: Why is it that I can't go into the office to give it to them?

Agent: There is no purpose.

Fred: I want to talk to them about it.

Agent: Well, there is nobody you can talk to about it. We're just employees here. Talk to your congressman if you have a problem. The forms are right here. It's a bureaucracy, you'll have to recognize that. (His tone was consoling.)

Fred: I understand that it's bureaucracy. I just don't see why I shouldn't be able to talk to, say, you, to people who work for the public.

Agent: Who's that?

Fred: Whoever it is who's working for the public, collecting the taxes.

Agent: What taxes?

Fred: They go to fight wars.

Agent: Why don't you write your congressman?

Fred: I've tried to do a number of things to contact my congressman. It seems to be pretty ineffective. I just wanted to talk to. . . .

Agent: It does you no good. . . .

Fred: Okay, thank you for your time. (This last is rather sarcastic.)

In contrast to the first incident, Fred did seem to want to engage the agent in conversation, and possibly win him over, or at least talk his way past. Fred was not too dominant, fairly positive, serious, and conforming (to the suggestions of the agent). If anything, the agent was even more outgoing and helpful. He noticed the form had not been signed, offered a pen, and was consoling about the nature of bureau-cracy. Had he also had training in a nonviolent role?

In fact, the police have been issued quite detailed instructions on arrest procedures for civil disobedience demonstrators. They are cautioned that time is not important in making arrests of demonstrators and there should be no haste. Civil disobedience teams are told that the policy of the police department is to recognize and respect the right to protest or demonstrate against a social custom or condition. Agents are cautioned to avoid picayune arrests because an arrest can be seen by the demonstrators as the successful climax of a demonstration and can be interpreted as a denial of the right to demonstrate. Thus an agent who has read the rules need not assume a position which is too dominant, negative, serious, or conforming in the first instance, although eventually he will have to assert his dominance in the interest of the conformity he has been trained to enforce, if the demonstrator persists in nonconforming behavior. In this case, Fred did not insist on going through the police line and the encounter seems to have ended in favor of the agent.

Summary

A search for the basic process categories of interpersonal behavior began in the 1920s with the observations of children. Beginning in the 1940s, the interest turned from individual categories to underlying dimensions. Major contributions to the dimensional approach have been made by Chapple, who demonstrated that action-silence (or dominant-submissive) was a central characteristic of interaction; Leary, who added the positive-negative dimension; and Bales, who fused two of Couch's factors to form forward-backward (serious and conforming vs. expressive and nonconforming) as a third dimension.

When Bales's third dimension is split into the original two, we have four dimensions of interaction process that are related to the four functional (AGIL) categories for content. When a group is working on a problem of Pattern maintenance (L), the conforming-nonconforming process dimension will be the most salient; when the problem is Integration (I), the positive-negative dimension will be salient; when the problem is Goal-attainment (G), the dominant-submissive dimension will be salient; and when the problem is Adaptation (A), the serious-expressive dimension will be salient.

Two sets of definitions for coding interaction on the four dimensions were given, one defining the two ends of each dimension and the other indicating seven points along each dimension. Two descriptions of the interaction between persons protesting the payment of war taxes in the United States and government officials illustrated the use of the ratings.

Chapter 3

Dramaturgical Analysis

The insight that "all the world is a stage" is no longer new. However, relatively few social scientists have chosen to use a dramaturgical approach in the analysis of interpersonal behavior. The work of Burke (1968) represents one approach. He notes that classic work on the theater has used the concepts of act, scene, agent, agency, and purpose to describe action on the stage and suggests that these same categories should illuminate the description of behavior in everyday life. Goffman (1959) set the pace in the use of dramaturgical concepts with his early work on the ways in which people try to manage the "impression" that they present to others, his analysis of behavior "backstage" and "on stage," and his insight that people often form "teams" in presenting themselves to others, as well as many more applications of concepts from the theater. However, his work is based on general descriptions and has not been concerned with the development of a more formal category system. MacCannell (1973) and Turner and Edgley (1976) have also used a dramaturgical approach, but mainly for the analysis of the structure of the action with little attention to the process as it flows from one scene to the next.

Although the formulations of Burke and Goffman include the concept of *role,* they do not stress the concept as a central part of their theories. In contrast, persons working within the theater do take this focus, since it is their business to help actors learn to take roles. Representative of the work in the theater is Stanislavski's book on *Creating a Role* (1961). He advises actors that they must be able to pour into their inner creative state a

AUTHOR'S NOTE: The analysis of the 1971 nonviolent protest in Washington is taken from my article "A Dramaturgical Analysis of Street Demonstrations, Washington, D.C., 1971 and Capetown, 1976," *Group Psychotherapy, Psychodrama, and Sociometry,* 33 (1980): 92-120. Copyright © 1980 by Heldref Publications, Washington, D.C. Reprinted by permission.

genuine sense of the life in their role in accordance with the given circumstances of the play. He also noted that each role has an emotional content or "inner tone." The external result is to play the role "on tears," "on laughs," "on joy," or "on alarm." Thus the role has two aspects, the amount of involvement or creative state, and the emotional tone.

The category system for dramaturgical analysis presented here was first used in the analysis of a psychodrama (Hare, 1976a) and then in the analysis of street demonstrations (Hare, 1980a). The present description of the system, together with an illustration of its use, is taken with minor changes from the second paper.

The dramaturgical category system is based on the work of Moreno and his followers, who developed psychodrama as a form of group therapy. In psychodramas, protagonists (patients) under the guidance of a director play out scenes from their own lives with the help of auxiliaries who take the parts of other persons, animals, objects, or ideas that are important in the situation. For Moreno, the basic elements in the psychodrama are the protagonist, director, auxiliary egos, audience, and stage or action area (Rabson, 1979).

As a psychodrama develops, it moves through a series of stages that have been identified by Blatner (1973: 49) as: (1) director's warm-up, (2) building group cohesion, (3) developing a group theme, (4) finding the protagonist, (5) moving the protagonist onto the stage, (6) action, (7) working through, and (8) closing. In terms of AGIL, stages 1-4 are part of the initial "L" as the theme and theme carrier are identified. Stage 5, moving the protagonist on stage, involves both "A" and "I" as information about the problem is given by the protagonist through an interview with the director and through "role reversal" in taking the part of auxiliary egos to indicate how they should act. Through this method, the roles that will be played in the psychodrama are established. Stages 6 and 7 are the "G" stages as the actual work is done. Ideally, in Stage 6 the protagonist experiences some emotional catharsis that makes possible some new insight into the problem (Moreno, 1946: 129). Stage 8 represents the final "L" stage as the protagonist is de-roled and returns to the group as group members share similar experiences that help to define "the meaning of all this" in terms of the larger society.

The various techniques that a director may use in the course of a psychodrama are taken from "real life" and so may be used for the analysis of ordinary behavior as well as that which is consciously staged. These techniques include the following (Rabson, 1979):

(1) Role reversal—An individual exchanges roles and physical positions with another person.

(2) Soliloquy—Verbalizing thoughts and feelings, often while turning the head to one side.

(3) Double—An auxiliary ego standing behind the protagonist to help express inner feelings.

(4) Mirror—An auxiliary ego presents the behavior of the protagonist, who steps out of the scene to observe.

(5) Auxiliary chair—An empty chair is used to represent a person, part of the self, value, or abstract symbol.

(6) Concretizing—A visual depiction of feelings and relationships.

(7) Maximizing—Increasing or exaggerating the emotional content of a communication or attitude.

Although the present system of analysis is based on psychodrama, it also applies to its derivative, "sociodrama." For Moreno, sociodrama dealt with a person as a role-player rather than as an individual personality. Whereas the psychodrama aimed at individual emotional catharsis and insight, the sociodrama "deals with social problems and aims at social catharsis" (Moreno, 1953: 88). Thus a protest demonstration, for example, is similar to a sociodrama. However, the mode of analysis and the techniques involved are the same.

By combining two category systems, the present system includes five categories for task behavior and four dimensions for social-emotional behavior. Since Moreno (1947: 57-58) emphasized the spontaneous and creative aspect of work (Haas, 1949: 227), the five task behavior categories represent five degrees of involvement and creativity. The definitions of the categories are taken from Stock and Thelen (1958: 193). Since they indicated only four levels of work, their second level has been split into two. This gives a better fit with the levels of creativity identified in Chapter 10. The five levels of involvement and creativity are:

(1) *Self oriented* (not in role)—work is personally need-oriented and unrelated to group work.

(2) *Stereotyped*—work is maintaining or routine in character.

(3) *Real*—work may involve attempting to define a task, searching for a methodology, or clarifying already established plans.

(4) *Involved*—work is group focused and introduces some new ingredient; active problem-solving.

(5) *Creative*—work is highly creative, insightful, and integrative. It often interprets what has been going on in the group and brings together in a meaningful way a series of experiences.

The four dimensions of social-emotional behavior are those given in Tables 2.1 and 2.2:

D—Dominant vs. submissive

P—Positive vs. negative
S—Serious vs. expressive
C—Conforming vs. nonconforming

Ratings of 1 through 7 are given within each of these dimensions as indicated in Table 2.2. For example, the ratings on the dominant-submissive dimension are:

7—Very dominant
6—Dominant
5—Slightly dominant
4—Neutral
3—Slightly submissive
2—Submissive
1—Very submissive

At the beginning of the analysis of an event, the transcript of the action can be divided into natural time periods, representing the "acts" in the "play." The end of an act usually involves a major change in personnel, location, or theme. "Scenes" within an "act" are marked by minor variations of the same type. The interaction in each scene is then coded, line by line if a transcript is available, or by summary ratings if there is only a general indication of the nature of the interaction. In either case an attempt is made to score the behavior for each role being played, that is, protagonist, director, auxiliary ego, or audience. Within a play one person may take many roles and the same role may be played by many persons. The uses of the various dramatic techniques of role reversal, soliloquy, double, and so on are also noted.

A major advantage of this type of dramaturgical analysis is the same as that for any comprehensive theory in that all aspects of interaction can and must be coded. As part of the record the observer must decide the role being played by each person at the time of each interaction and the major aspects of task and social-emotional activity must be noted. In any one play there may be several protagonists, each representing a different theme. If one role is primarily to counter the protagonist it can be designated the "antagonist." There may be different types of supporting members (auxiliary egos) who can be given separate designations. As with so many theories using the concept "role," it is left to the observer to make it clear how the concept is being applied in any particular instance.

The codes used here for a minimum set of roles are:

D—Director
P—Protagonist

N – Antagonist
S – Supporting member
A – Audience

When a person is doubling a role, the subscript of "2" is added to the symbol. Once this dramaturgical system has been used with a greater variety of situations, other conventions will undoubtedly develop.

The use of the dramaturgical approach is illustrated in the analysis of the following incident at a protest in Washington, D.C. in 1971 (Hare, 1980a: 94-103).

Washington, D.C., 1971:
An Incident at Selective Service

Nonviolent protest in the United States set a new record for militant action in Washington, D.C., in April and May 1971 with a series of marches, sit-ins, and other forms of confrontation including "mobile" tactics. The government responded by arresting 12,000 demonstrators. One of the more "classic" types of nonviolent confrontation was held at the Selective Service Headquarters from April 27 through 29. Part of that action included a conversation between Steve Stalonas and Inspector M of the Washington police force as Stalonas sought to cross a police line behind the headquarters building. This incident provides an opportunity to examine in detail the interaction between a nonviolent protestor and a typical counterplayer, a member of a policing force.

Several hundred demonstrators gathered in front of the national headquarters for the Selective Service System late in the morning on Tuesday, April 27. Some of them had spent the previous day talking with Curtis Tarr, director, and other Selective Service officials and had secured permission to come into the building and discuss their positions with employees there. The officials, however, had withdrawn this permission after hearing rumors that some individuals were planning to disrupt and destroy things once they got inside the building. Demonstration leaders responded by reemphasizing their pacifist orientation and pledging to keep nonviolent. They also asked the rest of the demonstrators to wait until mid-morning before coming to Selective Service headquarters, hoping that the continuing negotiations would have resulted in an open building by that time.

The decision of Selective Service officials on the morning of April 27 was to let some demonstrators enter the building to talk with employees, but only four at a time. The demonstrators agreed to send people in on this limited basis, but with the number gathered it was obvious that few of them would get inside the building that day. A restless feeling prevailed: the demonstrators seemed impatient and wanted to do something more. Using a portable sound system, some spoke of what they considered the proper action to take in the situation.

After several of these statements, Steve Stalonas took the microphone and declared, "We didn't come here to make speeches or to stand around listening to speeches. We came here to talk to Selective Service employees." He suggested that they circle around the building and call to employees to come out, and led a group that immediately began walking around the side of the building towards the back chanting, "Come out, come out, wherever you are! Come out, come out, wherever you are!"

Reaching the back of the building, they were met by police who warned them not to come any farther. The demonstrators asked why they were not being allowed to go around the building, but the officers gave no answer, simply reiterating the fact that they had established a police line. Some members of the group of demonstrators initiated a discussion with a police inspector regarding the arbitrariness of closing off the area when they had been acting peaceably; their conversation went on for about twenty minutes.

Eventually, Stalonas, who had led the group around, indicated that he would commit civil disobedience by breaking the line. There was no barricade, only a police officer bodily blocking the way, and Steve was reluctant to make a move that might be interpreted as assault upon the officer. Nevertheless, after more discussion, he did break the line by pressing against the officer's arm. He and three others who went into the off-limits area were arrested and charged with crossing a police line.

A Conversation Between
Steve Stalonas and Inspector M

A detailed description of the conversation between Steve Stalonas and Inspector M was prepared by Amelia Kritzer who had recorded the interaction on tape while I photographed the scene with color movie film (Kritzer, 1971). A sample of the transcript is given in Figure 3.1. The combination of a film and tape record has made it possible to code the interaction from a dramaturgical point of view with some confidence that the spirit of the original encounter has been maintained. Further, as a check on the accuracy of the typed transcript, a copy was sent to Inspector M in Washington. He was asked if there was anything about the transcript that might create difficulties for him should it appear in print without identifying him. There was no response.

With Steve Stalonas at the back of the Selective Service building were several other protestors who tended to act in chorus, calling out to the police from time to time. However the principal interaction was between Stalonas and the Inspector, with Ron Young of the Fellowship of Reconciliation acting as an intermediary at several points. As the

Role and Creativity Rating	Actor	Unit of Interaction	Four Dimensional Ratings
P5	Stalonas:	I still don't know your first name.	D5, P6, S5, C4
N3	Inspector M:	George.	D3, P6, S4, C4
P3	Stalonas:	George.	D4, P6, S4, C4
P4		I respect what you have to say,	D5, P5, S6, C4
P4		but it sounds a lot to me like what they said about 2,000 years ago.	D5, P2, S5, C4
P4		I have to do it (stay behind the police line) because that's what I've been told I have to do,	D5, P2, S5, C4
P4		not because I have thought it out for myself.	D5, P2, S5, C4
P5		I think the easiest way to make you think it out is by my crossing the line.	D6, P3, S6, C2
N4	Inspector M:	What do you gain by this, Steve?	D5, P6, S6, C6
P4	Stalonas:	What I gain by it is that you are going to have to arrest me.	D5, P5, S6, C2
N4	Inspector M:	What do you do about . . . (inaudible)	D4, P5, S5, C4
P4	Stalonas:	It's a simple act of sacrifice.	D4, P4, S6, C1
P4		I'm telling you that I don't believe in governments that say arbitrarily you can't be behind a building when you are not threatening anything.	D6, P2, S5, C1
N4	Inspector M:	Well, it's not an arbitrary decision.	D6, P3, S5, C7
N3		When we have these things going on, we sit down and we plan.	D6, P4, S5, C6
P3	Stalonas:	I understand,	D2, P5, S5, C5
P3		but the reason is to keep the peace,	D5, P3, S5, C4
P3		and there is nothing unpeaceful about what I am about to do,	D6, P2, S5, C2
P3		and I am going through.	D6, P2, S5, C1
P4		And if you arrest me, then you'll have to arrest me.	D6, P2, S6, C2
N5	Inspector M:	(bars the way by standing in front of Stalonas)	D7, P4, S5, C7
P4	Stalonas:	I don't want to get into assaulting an officer.	D5, P4, S6, C6
N4	Inspector M:	Well, I don't want you to either.	D4, P5, S5, C6
P4	Stalonas:	Okay, then I'm going to step through	
P3		and it's a simple matter.	D5, P4, S6, C2
N4	Inspector M:	(over his shoulder) Bring me up some more men here.	D6, PS, S7, C1 / D6, P4, S7, C7
S2	Officer:	(a police officer comes forward to block the way and Inspector M steps back)	

Figure 3.1

scene develops Stalonas establishes a relationship with the Inspector that includes the use of first names. Stalonas argues that the police line is not justified and that the proposed activity of discussing the war with the occupants of the building is legitimate. He concludes that if the police remain firm, he will have to cross the police line as an act of civil disobedience. At this point the Inspector calls up a younger policeman to block Stalonas's way. Stalonas makes it clear to the policeman what he is about to do and that he does not want to be charged with a felony for pushing past an officer. Eventually Stalonas pushes past, along with three others. They are arrested, booked, and taken to jail.

In the analysis of the transcript the unit to be scored is usually a simple sentence. However the unit may be only a single word or a bit of behavior if it represents a thought or action that seems complete in itself and would give enough information for another actor to respond. For example, the first statement in the transcript is by Stalonas who says: "I still don't know your first name." Using the four dimensional scheme for coding social-emotional behavior this sentence is coded as a 5 for Dominant (D5) since Stalonas is taking some initiative but is not insisting that the Inspector give his name. Nor does Stalonas seem to be so assertive in other ways that he should be rated as a 6 on Dominant. Part of this judgement is based on the tone of voice that was recorded by the tape recorder but does not appear in the transcript.

The same act is rated as 6 on the Positive vs. negative dimension (P6). Stalonas is showing "overt signs of friendliness." The rating of 5 for Serious vs. expressive (S5) is an indication that Stalonas is involved in the task. He is not treating it as a joke. However we also note that he is not dealing with a very serious issue at the moment. A rating of 4 is given on the Conforming vs. nonconforming scale (C4). The act does not clearly support conformity or nonconformity to the norms governing the interaction between Stalonas and the Inspector in that situation. If we are allowed a second thought we could code this act as a 5 on conformity or even a 6, depending upon the tone of voice, if we judged that the principal reason for the remark was to put pressure on the Inspector to give his first name. This would have the effect of urging the Inspector to conform to a norm introduced by Stalonas that the interaction should be on a "first name basis." As it was, the tone of voice suggested that the principal component of the act was on the Positive vs. negative dimension rather than on the Conforming vs. nonconforming dimension.

Thus we see that a great deal of information can be compressed into a single statement in a way that is similar to a dream that compresses many feelings into a single image. The response of the Inspector in giving his first name (which has been fictionalized in the account) indicates that he is slightly submissive (D3), quite positive (D6), and neutral on the Serious vs. expressive (S4) and Conforming vs. nonconforming (C4) dimensions.

After coding each act we find that in sum Stalonas has taken a stance that is Dominant without being overbearing, Positive, Serious, and Nonconforming. This matches the "ideal type" of nonviolent protestor described by Gregg (1935). The Inspector has been positive in response to Stalonas's positive behavior but has not, in this instance, been won over to Stalonas's position on the issue.

The codes for role and degree of involvement are given before the name of the actor and at the beginning of each act. In the sample of the interaction between Stalonas and Inspector M there are only two main roles, Stalonas is the theme carrier for the group or protagonist (P) and Inspector M represents the opposing theme, the antagonist (N). At the end of the transcript an officer comes forward as a supporting member (S). Most of the time both Stalonas and Inspector M are involved in what they are doing (level 4). There is some creativity at level 5 as an actor introduces a new idea or a new direction for action. The officer who came forward was responding to a routine command (level 2).

Two types of psychodramatic techniques were used: concretizing when Inspector M uses his body to bar the way and maximizing when he calls for more men.

This short transcript only illustrates how the category system is used. We will now go back over the entire incident to provide an analysis in dramaturgical terms.

Considering the incident behind the Selective Service building as a play it can be divided into five scenes. The first scene begins at levels 2 and 3 of involvement and includes the establishment of the police line by Inspector M and the response of the chorus of demonstrators (auxiliaries) who question the necessity of the police line. In Scene two Stalonas takes over as protagonist, questioning Inspector M with a counterpoint of comments by other demonstrators. Involvement reaches level 4 as the actors become more "warmed up" to the event. In scene three the height of personal involvement is reached as Steve and George move to a first name basis. The peak is reached when Stalonas says he will cross the police line but then falls off a bit as he goes over the point several times for the benefit of the young policeman who has been brought forward to block his way. Scene four includes the crossing of the police line and the arrests. It is quite short but provides the emotional catharsis and moment of insight for the demonstrators. As the arrests are made one of the demonstrators (auxiliaries) plays "Yankee Doodle" on a harmonica, thus indicating the "revolutionary" nature of the action. Just as MacCannell (1973: 64) has observed about "sit ins," that each "occupation" is a working model of a revolution, so it is apparent that the demonstrators define this encounter as part of a model of a revolution. In the fifth scene the four demonstrators who went through the police line are booked and taken away in a police van. The other demonstrators disperse.

The role of director during the event was shared by two persons. Initially Inspector M set the stage by arranging the police line and defining the action area. In the second scene, Ron Young, then secretary of the Fellowship of Reconciliation, takes a "third party" role as he tries to interpret Stalonas's remarks to Inspector M and points out to Stalonas that Inspector M is asking "fair" questions. This is similar to the behavior as a psychodrama director who may call for a particular line of action.

Throughout this action the additional auxiliary roles of demonstrators and police were played in a relatively undifferentiated way. The whole action contained only one major theme with two subgroups, demonstrators and police. Some events can be much more complex with several themes competing with each other.

Summary

The extent to which social interaction takes the form of a drama can be analyzed using a category system based on Moreno's work with psychodrama and sociodrama. First the action is divided into natural units to compare the overall development with the stages in a typical drama or psychodrama that include a warm-up, a series of scenes that reach a peak when the protagonist has some emotional catharsis followed by some insight into the basic problem presented in the drama, another scene or scenes devoted to working through the problem, and a closing period of "sharing" with members of the audience.

The role being played by each person in the drama was identified. A minimum set of roles includes: director, protagonist, antagonist, supporting member, and audience member. One person may play many roles and the same role may be played by several members.

The level of creativity evident in each person's action is rated on a five point scale as either (1) self-oriented, (2) stereotyped, (3) real, (4) involved, or (5) creative. The social-emotional behavior is rated on the four dimensions of Dominant-submissive, Positive-negative, Serious-expressive, and Conforming-nonconforming using seven-point scales.

The dramaturgical approach was illustrated by the analysis of an incident that was part of a protest demonstration against the Vietnam War in Washington, D.C. in 1971.

Chapter 4
Exchange Analysis

The theory of social exchange is a framework for analysis in social psychology, sociology, anthropology, and political science, characterized by the idea that social interaction can be viewed as the exchange of material or nonmaterial goods and services. It employs concepts analogous to those in economic analysis. Given the ubiquity of social exchange, Blau (1968: 453) has noted that it is not surprising that social philosophers such as Aristotle have been concerned with exchange ever since antiquity. Blau cites Adam Smith who wrote *The Theory of Moral Sentiments* in 1759 as a more recent but still early example of one who was intrigued by the varieties of exchange observable in much of social life. Anthropologists have described the patterns of exchange in small, relatively isolated groups of people. It is clear that ritual exchanges of gifts have more than economic implications. Not only are there norms for exchange but also "super norms" to tell what kind of exchange system is operating (Davis, 1975; Emerson, 1976).

Although many of the concepts used by persons writing about social exchange are similar, there is as yet no comprehensive set of propositions to which all would agree. Some, such as Emerson (1976: 336), argue that it is not a theory at all, but rather a frame of reference within which many theories, some micro and some macro, can speak to one another, whether in argument or in mutual support. Further, some critics, including Emerson, claim that there are basic problems with the few propositions that have been put forward. Some propositions require a degree of rationality

AUTHOR'S NOTE: The text beginning with the section on Langabaugh's exchange analysis through the chapter summary is taken from A. P. Hare and J. Mueller, "Categories for Exchange Analysis in Small Groups: With An Illustration from Group Psychotherapy," *Sociological Inquiry* (Publication of Alpha Kappa Delta, International Undergraduate Honor Society in Sociology), 1979, Vol. 49: 57-59, 60-63.

on the part of the human actor that is not always evident. Some propositions are essentially tautological statements and some propositions seem to depend on a form of psychological reductionism. For the reader who is interested in the weaknesses of social exchange theory, Shaw and Costanzo (1970), Mulkay (1971), Chadwick-Jones (1976), and others provide detailed critiques.

Some other theories are similar to exchange theory in their propositions but stress the outcome of the exchange rather than the process. For example, Newcomb (1953) and Heider (1958) were concerned with how people achieved "balance" in their relationships and Walster, Walster, and Berscheid (1978) were interested in the extent to which "equity" was involved. Most studies of cooperation and competition (Davis, Laughlin, and Komorita, 1976) and helping behavior (Darley and Latané, 1968) involve the analysis of some form of social exchange.

Basic Propositions

Blau (1968: 452) states that the basic assumptions of the theory of social exchange are that individuals enter into new social relationships because they expect to find them rewarding and that they continue with old relationships because they find them rewarding. A relationship is rewarding if there is some "profit" in it, that is, if the rewards exceed the costs. Usually there are several "options" open to the individual. A person must decide which option will maximize profit (maximizing) or which one is best in the given situation (satisficing). Overall, the individual expects "distributive justice," that is, people who give more should get more in return (Homans, 1974).

One of the earliest and clearest statements of the basic propositions in exchange theory was made by Homans (1974: 16, 22-23, 25, 29, 43):

(1) *The success proposition.* "For all actions taken by persons, the more often a particular action of a person is rewarded, the more likely the person is to perform that action."

(2) *The stimulus proposition.* "If in the past the occurrence of a particular stimulus, or set of stimuli, has been the occasion on which a person's action has been rewarded, then the more similar the present stimuli are to the past ones, the more likely the person is to perform the action, or some similar action, now."

(3) *The value proposition.* "The more valuable to a person is the result of his action, the more likely he is to perform the action." The value proposition is elaborated in

The rationality proposition. "In choosing between alternative actions, a person will choose that one for which, as perceived by

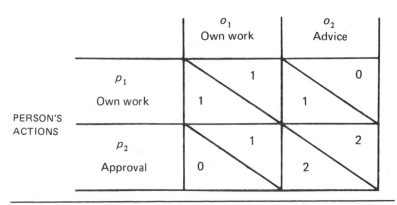

OTHER'S ACTIONS

Figure 4.1 Homans's Example of Exchange of Advice for Approval

SOURCE: G. C. Homans, *Social Behavior: Its Elementary Forms* (New York: Harcourt Brace Jovanovich, 1974), p. 54. Reprinted by permission of the publisher.

him at the time, the value, V, of the result, multiplied by the probability, p, of getting the result, is the greater."

(4) *The deprivation-satiation proposition.* "The more often in the recent past a person has received a particular reward, the less valuable any further unit of that reward becomes for him."

As an example of how social exchange between two persons can be seen in some detail, Homans (1974: 53-57) draws on the "payoff matrix" approach of Thibaut and Kelley to describe a situation based on the research of Blau. Blau's study concerned interpersonal relations in a government agency. Men were doing paperwork in an office, preparing reports. According to the rules of the government each man should do his own work, or if he needs help or advice he should consult his supervisor. Homans calls one of the men, who is new at the work and unskilled, "Person." He could do better if he received help from time to time but he does not want to confess his incompetence and thus damage his chances for promotion. The second man, whom Homans calls "Other," has worked in the office for some years, is skilled at the job, and has time to spare. In this case Person seeks advice from Other and gives him approval in the form of heartfelt thanks. This situation can be represented by the payoff matrix given in Figure 4.1.

Each of the men has two alternatives open to him. Other can either continue to do his work or stop and give Person advice; Person can either do his own work or listen to the advice and give Other approval. In the matrix, cell o_1p_1 represents the contingency in which each man continues his own work; o_2p_1, the contingency in which Person does his own work while Other gives advice unasked; $o_1 p_2$, the contingency in which Other gives no advice but Person gives approval anyway; and finally $o_2 p_2$ represents the contingency in which Other gives Person advice and Person gives Other approval.

The figures for the values of the rewards are arranged to show that Person values getting advice more than he does doing his own work. However doing his own work is not without value since that is what he is paid to do. If he asks for advice he forgoes the value of doing the work on his own. This forgone value is the cost to him of getting advice. Since he receives 2 units of reward in the form of increased work for giving approval to Other, his net reward is $2 - 1 = 1$.

In the same way it is assumed that Other sets a higher value on getting approval than he does on the rewards of doing his own work. Giving up his own work is the cost to him of getting approval. So the net reward for him is also $2 - 1 = 1$.

The matrix in Figure 4.1 includes two highly unlikely contingencies: $o_1 p_2$, when Other only does his own work but Person still gives him approval and $o_2 p_1$, when Person only does his own work but Other still gives him advice. The reason why these contingencies are unlikely to occur is that social exchange usually includes a minimum of three acts, a request by Person, an offer by Other, and a reward by Person. In this particular case, the exchange of advice for approval is preceded by Person's request for advice, without which Other is unlikely to offer advice spontaneously. Unless Person gets advice he is unlikely to give Other approval in return.

This example illustrates Homans's *value proposition* since each man chooses an action which gives a reward of greater value. It also illustrates the *stimulus proposition.* Other has presumably learned from past experience that a verbal request for advice is likely to be followed by approval, and Person has presumably learned that if he does not give approval Other will be less apt to honor his request for advice on the next occasion.

The payoff matrix approach can be expanded to include a number of Others to Whom Person might go for advice. These contingencies could be represented in additional columns of the matrix. Person could still choose the combination giving the highest net reward. However it becomes difficult for the theorist to represent the interaction of more than two persons on the two dimensional page of a book, so examples are rarely more complex than the one given above.

Some authors, such as Homans, are not especially concerned with the number of types of rewards that individuals can supply for each other. In the example above, Homans discussed the exchange of "advice" for "approval" without indicating whether these are "basic" types of rewards or commodities of social exchange or whether they are instances of one or

TABLE 4.1 Blau's Six Basic Types of Rewards

	Intrinsic	*Extrinsic*	*Unilateral*
Spontaneous Evaluations	Personal attraction	Social approval*	Respect-prestige†
Calculated Actions	Social acceptance*	Instrumental services*	Compliance-power†

*Entails investment costs for suppliers in addition to those needed to establish the social association.
†Entails the direct cost of subordination for suppliers.
SOURCE: P. M. Blau, *Exchange of Power in Social Life* (New York: John Wiley & Sons, 1964), p. 100. Reprinted by permission of the publisher.

more general classes of rewards. Other authors, such as Blau (1964) and Foa and Foa (1974) have suggested a limited set of categories that theoretically include all types of social rewards. Blau's (1964: 100) six basic types of rewards are given in Table 4.1.

In Table 4.1, Blau distinguishes two types of rewards, those that are given more-or-less spontaneously as a response to an act and those that depend upon some calculated action on the part of the supplier. The first two columns represent rewards that may be mutually supplied by two persons for each other, those that are intrinsic to the association between the individuals (such as personal attraction and social acceptance), and those that are extrinsic (such as approval of decisions or opinions and instrumental services). The third column represents rewards that are necessarily unilateral, which are manifest in the general respect for a person that bestows superior prestige on him and in the prevailing compliance with his requests that bestows superior power on him.

With reference to these six types of rewards Blau comments (1964: 100):

> The person who receives rewards from associating with another has an incentive to furnish inducements to the other to continue the association, and this is also the case if the rewards are spontaneous reactions that must not be bartered in exchange. Since it is rewarding for an individual to associate with others who accord him high respect, he is likely to provide sufficient inducements for them to continue the association unless he suspects them of simulating respect in order to obtain benefits from him. Positive evaluations of a person must not be bartered lest they cease to be accepted as genuine and thus lose their significance; but they do make social associations rewarding and worth some cost to the recipient and consequently enable the evaluator to reap some benefits from associ-

ating with him. Men sometimes take advantage of this fact and express approval of another in a calculating manner to obtain benefits from him in exchange, but this strategy of the sycophant can succeed only as long as its calculating intent remains hidden.*

Longabaugh's Exchange Categories

Although, as noted above, Blau described six categories that represent the basic set of rewards used in social exchange, he has not yet used these categories as a formal system for the analysis of act-by-act behavior in groups. Longabaugh (1963) proposed a set of categories and a method of analysis for exchange, but his system was designed for the observation of mother-child dyads and is not comprehensive enough for general use. However, it did provide the model for a system developed by Hare and Mueller (1979) which uses a set of content categories based on Parsonian functional (AGIL) theory (see Table 1.1 for definitions of categories). The analysis of part of a transcript of a group psychotherapy session, given at the end of this chapter, illustrates the use of the revised system.

Longabaugh (1963) saw two parts of exchange acts that could be coded: *resource salience,* the content, and *modality,* the way that the content is handled by the actors in exchange. Longabaugh divided salient resources into three classes: information, control (freedom and direction), and support. His six modalities were seeking, offering, depriving, accepting, ignoring, and rejecting. These three salient resources in six modalities provided eighteen categories plus a nineteenth, called "unscorable behavior." The nineteenth category included acts that were so incomplete as to be unclassifiable and residual acts that were not judged to constitute exchange.

The Longabaugh categories were specific to the requirements of observing and rating mother-child dyads, and Longabaugh commented on the limitations of his system for other purposes. He recognized, for example, that the ability to distinguish different kinds of information was important, and that support might have been divided into two classes of esteem and comfort. Splitting "support" into two types brings Longabaugh's categories more into line with the Parsonian categories:

Information:	subset of A;
Control:	subset of G;
Comfort:	subset of I;
Esteem:	subset of L.

Thus, while the Longabaugh and Hare-Mueller category systems are similar in their treatment of modality, the primary contribution of the revised category system is the employment of the AGIL concepts. The Parsonian categories are more exhaustive with regard to content, since the AGIL framework seems capable of subsuming all social behavior. The AGIL categories are also more specific in distinguishing content and more suitable for the task of analyzing group process.

The reliability of the Hare-Mueller category system should be very similar to Longabaugh's, since the same six modalities are used with a redefinition of the salient resources. Longabaugh (1963) used as a measure of reliability the percentage of act agreement (number of act agreements divided by the number of act agreements plus the number of act disagreements). Two observers were considered to agree on scoring a given act if they coded the same person as actor, the same modality for the act, and the same resource as salient in the act. Coding was done on the spot after training with written protocols. Longabaugh reported a median percentage of act agreement for 49 experimental sessions of 60 percent with a range of from 38 percent to 92 percent.

A Revised Notation for Exchange Analysis

In applying abstract exchange theory in a line-by-line analysis of a group psychotherapy transcript, we are interested in the content of the exchange (in terms of A, G, I, or L), the bids and requested bids for the commodity to be exchanged, who is "buying" and who is "selling," and whether the exchange is actually completed.

We might view the group as a corporation interested in collectively buying commodities. The group leader, in this case the therapist, is the chairman of the board, and the amount of influence that he wields in decisions about buying these commodities depends on his style of leadership and the degree to which any subgroups endorse or oppose his authority. In a psychotherapy group individual members are stockholders with a greater or lesser voting influence and also suppliers of the commodities, such as information and feelings, that the group is seeking.

The exchanges are notationally represented in the following manner. The person who is initiating the action, a call for bids or a bid, is represented by the first capital letter in the notation. The next capital letter represents the person who is the object of the action. The next letter, in lower case, represents one of the six modalities used in exchanges:

s — seeks
o — offers

d — deprives
a — accepts
i — ignores
r — rejects.

The last letter, a capital A, G, I, or L indicate the functional description of the commodity (for example):

A—money, information
G—power, control
I—influence, comfort
L—commitment, esteem

Often the last letter has a subscript to differentiate between different commodities, since content is important in exchange analysis.

A few lines from the transcript can be used for illustration:

Larry (Therapist):	What do you feel about this?
Bill (Patient):	Nothing.
Larry:	Nothing at all?

Larry is asking Bill for information about his feelings. This is coded as L B sA_2. The symbol A_2 is used because the information is of a certain type, as we shall see when we examine the transcript. Bill replies with a bid of information, B L oA_2. Larry does not accept this bid, L B rA_2. If Larry had accepted Bill's reply as valid, it would have been noted as L B aA_2. The whole interchange looks like this:

L B sA_2
B L oA_2
L B rA_2

Although at least three lines are necessary for an exchange to occur, the negotiation often goes on much longer for a single exchange.

Transcript Analysis

As an illustration of the use of exchange analysis of a session of group psychotherapy with alcoholics, we include part of a transcript from a group at the William Slater Hospital in Cape Town. The first section of the complete transcript does not contain proceedings of the group proper. Patients are coming in the whole time, and the topic of conversation concerns who should be in the group, or in the AGIL categories, L_i, since it is a basic question of membership, L, concerning the relations between the group members, I. It is almost as if an admission ticket is required for group membership, a ticket which consists of being either Larry's or Joy's patient. It is apparent that some people don't have a ticket, but Larry is not the ticket collector; he's just asking whether all the patients are sure they have the correct tickets. The ticket collector, as it turns out, comes in later. Steve comes in to announce that Charles and Fred don't have tickets for this group, but do have them for the downstairs group, and the two patients leave.

Larry begins to define the type of behavior that is expected from the patients in the group, or, we might say, to define the exchange contract for the session. He says that he and Joy know the patients better than anyone else, so that the patients should feel free to discuss personal problems, implying that the two therapists can offer sympathy and understanding (I) to the patients. Then Larry announces what commodities are and are not being sought for the group's collective buying. It turns out to be information (A). The unwanted information (denoted A-) is talking about drinking. What is being sought is A_1, information about problems leading up to and resulting from drinking; A_2, information about general feelings and concerns of the patient; and A_3, information about proposed solutions. The rewards to the patients which are to proceed from these solutions, and therefore presumably the criteria for judging the worth of the solutions, are getting well again, staying dry, and leading a satisfying life. By asking for this information, Larry has opened the floor for bidding.

In some cases, there is negotiation of the terms of this contract by the group, for we remember that it is the group as a whole which is buying these commodities, but in this group the contract put forward by the chairman of the board is accepted without comment, and George springs into action, perhaps a little prematurely, with a bid announcing that he has some A_1 to sell: information about the problems leading up to his drinking problem. In comes the ticket collector to interrupt the proceedings, but Willie resumes the proceedings by asking to know a little more about George's product (sA_1). Johann and Laurence signify their approval of the product (aA_1); they cast their votes to buy by elaborating on George's presentation (oA_1). In this they are showing solidarity with George, so we rate them as offering I to him (oI).

Laurence offers some A_3 to go along with George's A_1 (oA_3), but there is disagreement about this new contribution after George describes the proposed solution as "dutch courage" (oA_3), and Bill summarily dismisses the bid for A_3: "Forget about the dutch courage" (rA_3).

Finally Larry re-enters with a request for some information about George's original product A_1 (sA_1), his explanation that he drinks because he is shy. George doesn't appear to be able to elaborate much, and Willie comes in with his vote against buying George's product, saying that George doesn't show shyness in the group or in the hospital (rA_1): in effect, Willie offers George support or liking (oI) as a consolation for casting his vote against George's A_1.

This was not a final decision in the group, because the bartering for this single exchange goes on for quite a while after the point at which the transcript ends, but the group never did buy George's commodity.

In the middle section of the transcript Larry calls for A+ bids from third-week patients, and Willie and Bill announce that they are prepared to oblige. Larry concentrates on Bill and asks specifically for A_2 (information about feelings) and A_3 (information about proposed solutions). After an interlude of interchange for circumstantial information Bill reveals his commodity, A_3 (a proposed solution): he is going to divorce his wife. But Larry is more interested in getting A_2: what are Bill's feelings about the decision? Bill replies with what we label A_{20}, the zero signifying that Bill claims he has no feelings about it. Larry does not accept this last commodity (rA_{20}), but Bill persists in offering it (oA_{20}), in effect ignoring the rejection [$i(rA_{20})$], but also offering his oversupplied commodities A_3 and A− instead. Bill rejects Larry's A_{2E} (where "2E" is used to note the suggestion that Bill's emotions and his drinking problem are related) before it is even offered for the first time.

The negotiations fly for quite a while in this vein, with Larry seeking Bill's A_2 and offering A_{2E}, while Bill attempts to create a market for A_3, A−, and even a new commodity, A_{1A} (where "1A" is used to record the claim that he drank because he was simply fatigued).

Finally, Bill accepts Larry's proffered A_{2E}, but dealing continues as Larry perseveres in trying to secure some adequate A_2. When Bill signals that his only available A_2 commodity is A_{20}, Larry calls for help from Steve (L S sI+) and gets it (S I oI+).

Steve redraws the contract, offering to give I+, being able to "feel with (the patients)" (S P oI+) in exchange for A+, acceptable information (S P sA+). He reviews the negotiations (S B sA_2) and emphasizes that A_{20} is not good enough (S B rA_{20}), and suggests that Bill has a secret cache of A_2 (S B oA_2). What follows is an interesting negotiation concerning the relative values of the various commodities and has to do with the cybernetic hierarchy (see Chapter 1). Bill insists that his feelings, an L factor, and therefore highest in the cybernetic hierarchy, are of less importance than the divorce, which is an I factor, because it has to do with his social role (L < I). Steve asserts the opposite (L > I). Bill, in return, compares his feelings toward his wife and son with damaged tools, an analogy which would place them at the bottom of the hierarchy as A factors, and reasserts the supreme importance of the divorce decision (L = A < I).

The following excerpt from the transcript beginning with Bill's acceptance of Larry's offer and ending with the discussion of "damaged tools" illustrates the exchange notation:

L B oA$_{2E}$	Larry:	But are you, are you sure that it's not related to something which you might feel makes you really upset–say, feelings of rejection, or people not liking you, or things like that?
B L aA$_{2E}$	Bill:	You're right, I do.
L B sA$_2$	Larry:	I mean, can you identify things that really upset you?
B L oA	Bill:	O yes, absolutely, absolutely, it's there. More so in the last two-and-a-half years since I've been living there. Because I bought the property from the post office–through the post office, not that it makes any difference–but the rule states that if you invest in a house, you as the buyer, the owner, must live in that house, so of course I was forced to go and live with my family again. But before I was living away. Before I came here I was living in hotels, and I got out of that because I was drinking too heavily. But uh, these last two-and-a-half years plus, I've, I've had to uh, live here, to get the
B L oA$_{2E}$		uh subsidy. And in that time I've had time to analyze the attitude in the house. Underground friction, uneasiness.
L B sA$_2$,	Larry:	Have you had time to analyze yourself?
B L dA$_2$	Bill:	Myself? Well, myself is according to my history as was stated
B L oA$_3$		in my uh autobiography. But uh, having done what I had done, I bought the property, mainly for my son. And the
B L aA$_2$		attitude in the house has been such by him and his mother, I thought it was so stupid, and of course uh, I'm not insensitive to these things: these things upset me.
L B oA$_2$	Larry:	That's what I'm saying: you know you, they're really rejecting you, by saying that–
B L aA$_2$	Bill:	Yes.
L B sA$_2$	Larry:	And how d'you react to rejection?
BL oA$_2$	Bill:	I keep quiet, just keep quiet. Because I know what's going to
BL oA$_3$		happen. They think I'm treating that wrongly. I've already spoken to them. The subject remains the same. So they've had their warning. But I didn't tell them that "there's going to be quite a change in this house.' They don't answer. No
B L oA$_{20}$		temper, no nothing. I can't I can't, I have, I can't be bothered having a temperament, going into a temper for that, even when I was drinking. I couldn't be bothered. It's a waste of energy.
L S sI+	Larry:	I, I'm sure for instance Steve would, would disagree with you completely about that. Steve, what do you think?
S L oI+	Steve (nurse):	Yah, (Bill), you know, um, I've once thought, well at the
Contract:		beginning, you know, when somebody talks, and I can feel
S P sA+		with them, you know, and, really live myself into the situa-
S P oI+		tion, and you seem to just on a superficial level, just pour out, and don't really give anything of yourself, you know,
S B sA$_2$		and um I, I do feel it is healthy to express your feelings and it's, it's, it's not good to keep it inside. And I think that that's what you're doing, you know, you're saying, 'O,
S B rA$_{20}$		they're rejecting me,' and, and you know, 'I don't feel very
S B oA$_2$		much about it,' and in reality I think you do feel a hell of a lot.

B S aA$_2$	Bill:	I do feel it. But I know how I am going to end it. And then
B S oA$_3$		I'll feel better. [L $<$ I.]
S B sA$_2$	Steve:	But can you share some of your feelings with us?
B S dA$_2$	Bill:	I don't think it's going to uh help in this sense, because I've made my decision, and after all to hear it.
S B sA$_2$	Steve:	I think so, I think it's going to help you quite a lot, because the feelings are still going to be there, you know, it's unresolved, it's there. [L $>$ I.]
S B rA$_3$		You must work with them, otherwise you know you're not going to stop it just by divorcing your wife.
	Bill:	I have one method of living: that if a tool is damaged, there's only one way for it—throw it away. It's of no use to me, or to my life. [L $<$ I.]
B S oA3		And if my marriage is damaged, and my relationship with my son is damaged—
S B sA$_2$	Steve:	How do you feel about that, (Bill), you know you—
B S oA$_2$	Bill:	That I don't like. That, that's going to last longer than anything else.
S B sA$_2$	Steve:	Hmm. What effects does it, has it got on you—how does it make you feel inside?
B S oA$_2$	Bill:	Well, I'm terribly disappointed, and uh it does work on me.
B S oA$_3$		But uh, that is something I just have to live with. I can't make anybody like me or love me if they don't want to.
S B sA$_3$	Steve:	Have you ever tried?

Steve perceptively pursues the angle of the son, which touches a nerve, and succeeds in getting Bill to express some real emotions about the relationship to his son. But Bill reverts for a while to offering more A$_3$. When he returns to the A$_2$ after a long monologue, Steve reinforces the behavior and clinches the exchange as outlined in his contract, giving I+ for A$_2$. At this point the therapy really begins, and Steve begins to explore with Bill the ramifications of his feelings toward wife and son. This runs into a snag when Bill refuses to disclose a particularly important fact about himself which he feels it would be threatening to reveal. Steve appeals to the group at large without success to bring pressure on Bill, and then Larry steps back in and observes that individual facts are not as important as the expression of feelings, and says he does not want to damage the exchange so arduously set up for the sake of relatively unimportant information.

The exchange pattern proceeds, with Bill offering his A$_2$, and Steve supplying his I+ to fulfill his side of the bargain.

The "typical ending" of this psychotherapy group might be seen as an audit held after bidding and buying has been closed down, to determine what kind of profit the interested parties have secured. Larry refers back to the original contract, one of the clauses of which indicated that patients would gain the reward of feeling better in return for the cost of information, when he asks if Bill is feeling better. Bill indicates that he has turned a small profit, and Larry tries to reinforce the exchange by approving Bill's expression of feelings.

The whole analysis, likened to an auction in a corporation, may seem rather metaphorical. But the simile itself is more an illustrative terminology to aid in understanding the exchanges than a concept crucial to the category system or the theory of social exchange. Terms like "admission tickets," "bidding," "buying," "commodities," and "auditing," although heuristically adequate, could be exchanged for duller terminology, but this would increase the reader's cost in tedium, and probably terminate the exchange.

The Profit in Exchange Analysis for Group Therapists

Question: What are the uses of the category system for staff conducting therapy groups?

Answer: It is a systematic way of looking at social behavior, and can help explain why some therapeutic approaches are more successful than others.

Question: Why, for example, is Steve's approach in the transcript fairly successful?

Answer: Because he states explicitly for the patient what he is going to do. The contract calls for an exchange of information for support. When he receives information from the patient, he sees to it that he gives support. The behavior is reinforced and trust in the patient-therapist exchange relationship is built for the future. It is not expected that the staff member keep a running coding of the exchanges, but the system helps him or her to question whether or not the patient is receiving enough profit to continue with the therapy.

By noting the exchanges a person is willing to make, one becomes aware of the person's hierarchy of values, what seems to be potentially the most rewarding outcome, and what are acceptable costs. This in turn will indicate that person's willingness to take on a new role, such as that of the "good patient," or to give up an old one, such as that of "alcoholic." Since each role involves a set of rights and duties it is important to be able to judge the extent to which an actor will accept the rewards and bear the costs.

Summary

Exchange theory is based on the idea that social interaction is similar to economic behavior in that it involves an exchange of material or non-material goods and services. Within the social-psychological literature, the major contributions to exchange theory have been made by Thibaut and

Kelley (1959), who used a "payoff matrix" approach; Homans (1974), who focused on informal groups; and Blau (1964), who was interested in exchanges within organizational settings. Persons enter into new relationships or continue with old ones as long as there is some profit as a result of the transaction.

Although Blau and Foa and Foa (1974) have provided lists of the major categories of "goods and services" that are involved in social exchange, they have not used them for systematic act-by-act analysis. Longabaugh developed a set of categories for both the content and the process of exchange for the analysis of mother-child interaction. Since his content categories are included in the more general set of four functional categories (AGIL), a revision of his system can be used for exchange analysis in any setting. The content categories are A,G,I, and L and the process categories are seeks (s), offers (o), deprives (d), accepts (a), ignores (i), and rejects (r).

The notation for exchange analysis was illustrated with the excerpt from the transcript of a group therapy session at a hospital for alcoholics.

PART II

GROUP PROCESS AND STRUCTURE

This section provides an analysis of two aspects of group process (development and social control) and two aspects of group structure (the network of interpersonal choice and the relationship of roles) in terms of one or more of the perspectives presented in Part I. As groups develop over time, the nature of the task activities and the relationships of members with each other tend to change following some identifiable patterns. At each stage the processes of social control are central if the members are to work together as a group to deal with the functional problems of that stage. In relation to group structure, members develop expectations for each other's behavior on the informal basis of the network of interpersonal choice or on the more formal basis of roles that may be assigned or develop in response to task or social-emotional problems.

AUTHOR'S NOTE: The section on the functional analysis of group development and the reviews of the work of Tuckman and of Mann are largely taken from my article "Theories of Group Development and Categories for Interaction Analysis," *Small Group Behavior* 4, 3: 259-304, Copyright © 1973 Sage Publications, Inc.

Chapter 5

Group
Development

Until the 1950s—with the exception of a few writers such as Coyle (1930)—there was little recognition of stages in group development. In some cases one can go back to a "classic" piece of research, such as the Western Electric Studies (Roethlisberger and Dickson, 1939) where a fairly complete transcript was made and discover that the group of girls in the "Test Room Study" together with their nondirective male observer went through stages of development that look very much like the stages in a typical "self-analytic" or "sensitivity training" group (Hare, 1967).

The first studies of group development that caught the attention of a number of group observers, leaders, and therapists were those of Bales (1950), who described the problem-solving sequence within a single meeting and the development of a status hierarchy over a series of meetings, and Bion (1961) who saw groups moving back and forth between different emotional states. Their work along with that of about 50 others was summarized in the first major review by Tuckman (1965). This review is based on studies from four fields: therapy groups, training groups, natural groups, and laboratory groups. From these studies Tuckman abstracted four stages of group development to which he has since added a fifth terminal stage (Tuckman and Jensen, 1977).

AUTHOR'S NOTE: Various sections of this chapter are reprinted with permission of Macmillan Publishing Co., Inc. from *Handbook of Small Group Research* by A. Paul Hare. Copyright © 1976 by The Free Press, a division of Macmillan Publishing Co., Inc.—"Tuckman's Four Stages of Development," from pp. 100-101; "Mann's Analysis of Member-Leader Relationships," from pp. 106-109 (condensed); "A Functional Analysis of Group Development," from pp. 110-111 (condensed).

The Section on the Antillean Institute of Social Science is taken from A. P. Hare, F. Carney, and F. Ovsiew, "Youth Responds to Crisis: Curacao," in A. P. Hare and H. H. Blumberg (eds.) *Liberation Without Violence* (London: Rex Collings, Ltd., 1977), pp. 221-224, 229. Reprinted by permission.

After Tuckman began his review, a series of studies were published by persons who had worked with Bales at Harvard as leaders of "self-analytic" groups of students who were taking a course on group dynamics. Some of the principal theories covered by Tuckman as well as those appearing later, up to 1974, are included in a review that forms the basis for some of the material in this chapter (Hare, 1973b, 1976b: 88-112). During the period since 1974, additional articles on group development have appeared (Adelson, 1975; Cottle, 1976; Farrell, 1976; Lundgren, 1977; Shambaugh, 1978).[1] As examples of some of the theories of group development that are incorporated in the present theory, the work of Tuckman (1965), Mann, Gibbard, and Hartman (1967), and Shambaugh (1978) will be summarized. These will be followed by a set of hypotheses concerning group development in terms of functional theory with three illustrations, first some incidents from the voyage of the raft *Acali* in 1972, second a description of a workshop for training in nonviolent action held in 1970, and third the preparations for a summer institute for social science held on the island of Curacao, Netherlands Antilles, that same year.

Tuckman's Four Stages of Development

Tuckman first abstracted his theory from some 26 studies of development in therapy groups. The task in these groups was to help individuals deal with personal problems. The groups typically contained from five to fifteen members and a therapist and existed for a period of three months or more. The developmental data for groups of this type consist of the observations of the therapist and those professional observers who may be present, usually as trainees. The data are highly anecdotal in nature and reflect the clinical biases of the observers. The accounts are usually formulated after the fact and based on the observation of a single group. Tuckman then went on to show how this same theory might be applied to training groups and later to laboratory groups and those observed in natural settings.

Each of the four major stages in group development which Tuckman describes are divided into two aspects: (1) *group structure,* where he describes patterns of interpersonal relationships—that is, the way in which members act and relate to one another as persons; and (2) *task behavior,* where he describes the nature of the work being done by the group. This distinction between task and social-emotional behavior had earlier been proposed by Bales (1953) and others. The four stages in group structure are, briefly, testing and dependence, intragroup conflict, development of group cohesion, and functional role-relatedness. The four stages of task activity are orientation and testing, emotional response to task demands, discussing oneself and other group members, and emergence of insight. Each of these stages as it applies to a therapy group can be summarized as follows:

Stage 1

Group structure: Testing and dependence. An attempt by group members to discover what behaviors are acceptable in the group, based on the reactions of the therapist. Members look to the therapist for guidance and support in this new and unstructured situation. (With antisocial individuals, there may be a prestage of resistance, silence, and hostility.)

Task activity: Orientation and testing. At this stage, the group members make indirect attempts to discover the nature and boundaries of the task. These attempts are evident in the following kinds of activity:

(1) Discussion of irrelevant and partially relevant issues
(2) Discussion of peripheral problems
(3) Discussion of immediate behavior problems
(4) Discussion of symptoms
(5) Griping about the institutional environment
(6) Intellectualization

Also, group members make more direct attempts at orientation toward the task as illustrated in:

(1) Search for the meaning of therapy
(2) Attempts to define the situation
(3) Attempts to establish a proper therapeutic relationship with the therapist through the development of rapport and confidence
(4) Mutual exchange of information
(5) Attempts to overcome suspicion and fear of the new situation

Stage 2

Group structure: Intragroup conflict. Group members now become hostile toward one another and toward the therapist as a means of expressing their individuality and resisting the formation of group structure.

Task activity: Emotional response to task demands. Emotionality is expressed by the group members as a form of resisting the techniques of therapy or of sensitivity training groups which require that they "expose" themselves. They also challenge the validity and usefulness of the training.

Stage 3

Group structure: Development of group cohesion. Group members accept the group and accept the idiosyncrasies of fellow members. Harmony is of the maximum importance, and task conflicts are avoided to ensure harmony.

Task activity: Discussing oneself and other group members. The self and other personal characteristics are discussed. Information is acted on in such a way that alternative interpretations of the information can be made. The openness of members to each other is characteristic.

Stage 4

Group structure: Functional role-relatedness. The group members work together on the task with a minimum of emotional interaction. This is made possible by the fact that the group as a social entity has developed to the point where it can support rather than hinder the task processes through the use of function-oriented roles.

Task activity: Emergence of insight. Group members show insight into their own problems, an understanding of their own abnormal behavior, and, in many cases, modifications of their behavior in desired directions.

Mann's Analysis of Member-Leader Relationships

Mann is primarily concerned with the way members of a training group relate to the leader. This can occur at four levels, ranging from a direct expression of feeling toward the leader to remarks in which the reference to the member may be disguised or symbolized although the reference to the leader may be direct.

Once the level of inference has been noted the appropriate content category is selected from the list given in Table 5.1. The content categories of the member-to-leader scoring system can be looked at as three separate systems that are used simultaneously. Of the 16 categories, eight describe the affective response a member may have to the leader; three describe feelings that are activated by the leader's status in the authority structure of the group; and five describe how the member feels about self in relation to the leader. These three approaches to the member's feelings are referred to by Mann as areas of (1) impulse, (2) authority relations, and (3) ego state.

The behavior of the leader is also scored using the 16 categories, although the observer does not ask what feeling is being expressed toward

TABLE 5.1   Mann's Member-to-Leader Scoring System Categories

Area	Subarea	Category
Impulse	Hostility	1. Moving against
		2. Resisting
		3. Withdrawing
		4. Guilt inducing
	Affection	5. Making reparation
		6. Identifying
		7. Accepting
		8. Moving toward
Authority relations		9. Showing dependency
		10. Showing independence
		11. Showing counterdependency
Ego state	Anxiety	12. Expressing anxiety
		13. Denying anxiety
		14. Expressing self-esteem
	Depression	15. Expressing depression
		16. Denying depression

SOURCE: Richard D. Mann, Graham S. Gibbard, and John J. Hartman, *Interpersonal Styles and Group Development* (New York: John Wiley & Sons, 1967), p. 42. Reprinted by permission of the publisher.

the members. Instead, Mann records the leader's reflection of members' feelings back to the group.

The 16 categories and four levels of inference were applied to the interaction in four classroom groups conducted at the Harvard Summer School in 1961-1963. They were all sections of the Social Relations 120 course. Before carrying out his analysis of the process of development in the four groups, Mann subjected the 20 dimensions to the statistical method of factor analysis to see if a smaller number of underlying dimensions could be used to describe the behavior; that is, he wished to know if the various categories fell into a smaller number of clusters. For this purpose, he converted the amount of behavior in each category for each member of the groups in each session to percentages. This unit of one member for one session he called a *performance*. A performance was only included in the analysis if he had recorded at least 20 acts to the group member for that session. This gave him a sample of 430 performances. As a result of the factor analysis, Mann identified six basic factors (see Table 5.2).

Before using these six factors in the description of group development, Mann added a description of the conceptual framework that emerged from

TABLE 5.2   Mann's Factor Patterns for Member Performances

Factor I: Relations with the leader as analyst
          I+: Enactment
          I−: Dependent complaining

Factor II: Relations with the leader as authority figure
          II+: Rebellion
          II−: Loyalty

Factor III: Relations with the leader as manipulator
          III+: Counterdependent flight
          III−: Resistant complaining

Factor IV: Relations with the leader as audience
          IV+: Relating to the leader as colleague
          IV−: Concern with inner distress

Factor V: The effect of the leader on the ego state of the member
          V+: Anxiety
          V−: Depression

Factor VI: Commitment to the member-leader relationship
          VI+: Emotional involvement
          VI−: Emotional neutrality

SOURCE: Richard D. Mann, Graham S. Gibbard, and John J. Hartman, *Interpersonal Styles and Group Development* (New York: John Wiley & Sons, 1967), p. 187. Reprinted by permission of the publisher.

his clinical study of the groups. He saw four themes occurring with considerable regularity: nurturance, control, sexuality, and competence (Mann, Gibbard, and Hartman, 1967: 73). His theory of group development in its simplest form is that groups pass through phases of development in this same order. That is, group members begin in a dependent stage concerned with problems of nurturance, then move to a struggle with the leader as they work on problems of control, then to more concern with intermember relations and the problem of sexuality, and finally arrive at a stage of mature work that they do with competence. In general, these phases are similar to the four phases described by Tuckman (1965).

Using examples from the transcripts of group meetings and graphs showing the trends in activity on each of the six factors over the life of the four training groups, Mann goes on to show the relationships between the four themes, the six factors, and other theories of group development. In brief, the primary factor associated with the first theme of nurturance is Factor II: relations with the leader as an authority figure. The second theme, control, is associated with Factor III: relations with the leader as manipulator. The third theme, sexuality, is associated with Factor IV: relations with the leader as audience. Finally, the fourth theme, competence, is associated with Factor I: relations with the leader as analyst.

Mann finds that four themes are sufficient to account for most of the process of group development. In his final analysis, Mann does add a fifth phase to emphasize a type of activity that he feels previous observers have overlooked. Just after the period of initial complaining and nurturance, group members appear to take over the group for a brief period of work at the task of group and case analysis. Since the group has not yet worked out its basic problems, this period of work cannot be sustained. For this reason, Mann called this period one of "premature enactment." In his final presentation of a theory of group development (Table 5.3) Mann places the themes of control and sexuality in the middle phase of "confrontation" and stresses a final phase of "separation and terminal review."

Shambaugh's Observations on Emotionality and Task Activity

Shambaugh (1978), a psychiatrist, does not present data for a specific group or set of groups; but from the biographical note with his article, one can infer that he is drawing on his experience in group therapy. However, since most of the principal theories of group development have been based on observations of therapy or therapy-like groups, this should not limit the generalizability of the hypotheses as long as one keeps in mind the nature of the "task" in the therapy group.

In common with many theorists before him, Shambaugh distinguished two aspects of behavior in groups: emotionality and task activity. Shambaugh (1978:298) sees emotionality as "a series of damped oscillations describing the fluctuating feelings of closeness and separateness of the members as they approach psychological individuation." In his journal article, Shambaugh presents a graph with *time* on the horizontal axis and *closeness* on the vertical axis. The graph depicts the fluctuations of closeness over time starting at zero, rising at an angle of about 45 degrees to a relatively high level of closeness, remaining at that level for a brief period, then plunging to a level of separateness as far below the zero point as the closeness was above. After a brief period of maximum separateness, the graph rises once more, again crossing the zero point until it reaches a level of closeness that is not as high as the first peak. This is followed by another plunge, but not as low as the first. As the graph rises again it stops, indicating that if the series were continued the members' emotionality would continue to oscillate but with ever decreasing fluctuations.

Shambaugh cites Bales's (1953) earlier description of the "equilibrium problem" as a similar oscillation. Bales had observed a tendency for group members to swing back and forth between attempts to complete the task, thus generating interpersonal hostility and distance, and attempts to main-

TABLE 5.3 Mann's Subgroup Characteristics by Phase

Phase	Dominant Subgroups	Deviant Subgroups
Initial complaining	Dependent complaining Loyal compliance Counterdependent heroics Self-sufficiency	Enactment in the service of autonomy
Premature enactment	"The sensitive ones" Withdrawal and denial "The accepting enactors" "The heroic enactors"	Disappointment and resentment
Confrontation	Rebellion and complaining (including "the spokesmen") Independence Anxiety and withdrawal	"The heroes"
Internalization	Enactment and work	"The scapegoats"
Separation and terminal review	Depression and manic denial Personal involvement Complaining abdication of responsibility	

SOURCE: Richard D. Mann, Graham S. Gibbard, and John J. Hartman, *Interpersonal Styles and Group Development* (New York: John Wiley & Sons, 1967), p. 187. Reprinted by permission of the publisher.

tain the group and satisfy the needs of the members, thus generating positive behavior and closeness.

Shambaugh provides a second graph to depict the generation of group culture (that is, the mainly implicit, internalized totality of group-relevant points of view, understandings, practices, and norms). As the group builds its culture, the leader becomes less and less central. With *time* on the horizontal axis and *culture* on the vertical axis, the second graph shows an increase in culture at about a 30 degree angle, beginning with time zero, to a point where it levels off, then rises more sharply to another point where it levels off, and again rises even more sharply. The graph stops before a third plateau is reached, presumably to indicate continuous growth over the life of the group. This stepwise development of culture is related to the oscillations in emotionality. "During the phases of emotional closeness and positive feeling, understanding and agreement are facilitated, identification and learning are rapid, and cooperative task effort increases, whereas the opposite trends appear during negative fluctuations and cultural elaboration slows" (Shambaugh, 1978: 291-292).

There is no indication on the two graphs of how they fit together in an exact way. Presumably they are meant to illustrate visually the idea that "task activity and culture building occur principally during phases of positive feeling and emotional closeness" (Shambaugh, 1978: 294) and that work on the task generates negative feelings that require the group to turn to social-emotional problems until the negative feelings have been handled.

A Functional Analysis of Group Development

The basic outline of the theory of group development presented here was suggested by Effrat and tested in the field in an analysis of a small regional development planning board in the Philippines (Hare, 1968), then by comparing it with other theories (Hare, 1973b), and further elaborated with field experience in Curacao, Netherlands Antilles (Hare and Blumberg, 1977: 281-282). In terms of the AGIL categories given in Chapter 1, the typical sequence of development in small groups seems to be L-A-I-G with a terminal stage of L.

When the AGIL categories are applied to the description of a learning group, such as a classroom group, the forces at work seem to be as follows: the work of the group requires that the purpose of the group be defined (L), that new skills be acquired (A), that the group be reorganized so that the members can try out new skills without being too dependent on the leader (I), and that the group members work at the task (G). Finally, there is a terminal phase when the group is disbanded. The group returns to L to redefine the relationships between the members and the group, to distribute the remaining resources, and to consider the meaning of the group experience for the individual member.

The amount of time the group spends in each phase is determined by the activity of the leader (direction or nondirection) and by the skills and emotional strengths of the members. Presumably, the leader is ready for each stage at the outset, having been through the stages before. However, members come to the group with different degrees of problem-solving skills or preferences for different emotional modalities; the usual bases for the formation of subgroups. If the subgroup with the appropriate skills and emotional state is large enough or strong enough, it can carry the whole group through that phase. If not enough members of the group are ready for a particular stage, more intervention by the leader may be necessary. Some groups never progress beyond the early stages and some recycle through the same stage several times before gaining enough closure on that stage to move on to the next.

The assumption that the group moves from phase to phase when a subgroup or leader is able to carry the movement needs further documentation in research, since many of those who propose theories of group development do not discuss the *process* of development in any detail; rather they simply *observe* that one phase follows another. A typical comment is that of Schutz (1958: 171) concerning the affection phase: "Finally, following a satisfactory resolution of these problems of control, problems of affection become focal." Schutz does not tell us how the problems of control become resolved or by what process the group moves on to the next phase. However, it may not require much justification to assert that a group will face special problems at the beginning and at the end of its life. For example, at the beginning of a training group, when the leader fails to be assertive, Bennis and Shepard (1956: 420) observe: "The ambiguity of the situation at this stage quickly becomes intolerable for some." Or Mills (1964: 78), describing the termination of a group, says: "The fact of separation forces a complex set of demands and issues."

With the L-A-I-G sequence in mind, we can now go back to Tuckman's and Mann's descriptions of group development to observe the fit between their phases and the four functional categories. Tuckman's Stage 1—orientation and testing—is primarily L although it includes A as members learn about the proper therapeutic relationship and exchange information. Stages 2 and 3 are both parts of I, as members clarify the roles to be played in the group. Stage 4 is G, as members actually work together on the task. In a later article, Tuckman and Jensen (1977) added a fifth, terminal stage, that is, the terminal L.

Mann's first stage of "initial complaining" is primarily the L stage as group members seek to define the meaning of the situation. The second stage of "premature enactment" reflects the members' first attempts to use their new skills in the analysis of interpersonal behavior (A phase). The enactment is "premature" because the members have not yet reorganized themselves in a way that frees them from dependence on the trainer. This is done in the next phase of "confrontation" (I). The next-to-last phase of "internalization" is G, as members carry out the work of group analysis. This is followed in Mann's scheme by a final phase of "separation and terminal review," which brings the group again to L.

Phases Within Phases

Although the basic outline of four phases (LAIG) with a terminal stage of L may be enough for many purposes, it is also possible to identify the same sequence of phases (that is, L-A-I-G) within each of the major phases; thus providing a better understanding of how groups move from one phase to the next, as well as providing a way to integrate the observations of Shambaugh (1978) on emotionality and task activity.

The phases within the phases are most easily seen when the group requires some special equipment for its task and when the nature of the work requires clear role differentiation. Without going into all the details of the adventure, incidents from the voyage of the raft *Acali* from the coast of Africa to the coast of Mexico in 1972 (Genovés, 1979) can be used to illustrate each of these subphases. Although I did not sail with the raft, I was on hand as a participant observer during the preparations for sailing in Madrid and Las Palmas and during the debriefing at Cozumel on the coast of Mexico and the welcome in Mexico City at the end of the voyage (Hare, 1974).

In this case, as in many, the idea of the exercise began with one person. The development of the idea by one individual, or by a small set of persons who may become a subgroup of the "founders" in the eventual small group (or large group for that matter) can be thought of as either a "pre" stage of L or as a third level of analysis within the L stage (that is, the stages within the L_1 stage). Santiago Genovés, the originator of this particular expedition, had already served as a crew member on two previous voyages of rafts over the same route, RA I and RA II, led by Thor Heyerdahl (1972), and already had the basic information for the idea. Since the fact that one could drift on a raft from Africa to Mexico had already been established, Genovés had to give a new meaning to the voyage.

As the idea occurred to him while the Vietnam war was in progress, he decided that he would bring together on the raft representatives of groups that might otherwise be in conflict as a demonstration of the possibilities for peaceful coexistance of Black and White; Muslim, Christian, and Jew; and Old and New World. Unfortunately, by the time the expedition was ready to begin the Vietnam war no longer occupied the public mind. So the voyage was now labeled a scientific expedition to study "sexual behavior, et cetera, et cetera." In the news conferences at the beginning of the voyage, it was never too clear what the "et cetera" stood for, although it presumably included taking samples of pollution in the sea. However the press seems to have gotten the message since as the raft sailed from Las Palmas one British newspaper carried the headline: "Sex Raft Sails."

One visible part of the L stage involved the final selection of the crew of 11 for the voyage. This took place at a convent in Madrid. It required several types of supplies and equipment: the convent and psychological tests, for example. The provision of these would be classified as L_a (or a subphase of A within the L phase). Also, special roles were needed for the selection process: doctors, psychologists, graphologists, and so on. These would be classified as L_i (or part of the subphase of I within the L phase).

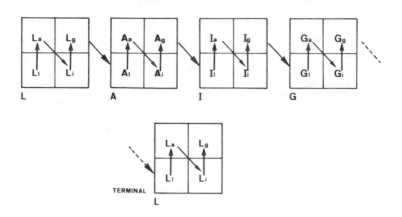

Figure 5.1 Subphases of Group Development

Thus the idea of selection of the crew (an L_1 activity) required the provision of special equipment (L_a) and the formulation of special role relationships (L_i) to carry out the actual selection (L_g).

Once the crew had been selected, they needed a raft that was fully equipped. Part of this A activity had been completed in England where the raft had been designed and built before being shipped to Los Palmos; however, a distinct A phase was required to complete the work and ready the raft for the sea voyage. This involved a whole set of ideas for construction and provisions (A_1), special tools (A_a), ship's carpenters and other specialized roles (A_i), and of course the work of fitting it all together (A_g).

While the A activity was in progress, the I activity was underway as various crew members were given an orientation for their roles on board the raft (I phase). The final G phase was the actual voyage, with the terminal L phase taking place at Cozumel where the group was debriefed by psychiatrists and matters of physical and mental well-being attended to before the group traveled to Mexico City to meet the press and to speculate about the meaning of the experience for their future lives.

If I were presenting this as an actual case, rather than an illustration, details of the subphases within the I and G phases could be added. As it happened, the major role conflict within the group occurred just at the end of the I phase, where it seems most likely that the "revolution within the revolution" will occur, as will be noted in the discussion that follows.

The general schema showing the progress through the phases within phases is set out in Figure 5.1. The movement to any major phase is from the subphase "g" in the prior phase. Thus once a group has completed its definition of its overall purpose and secured the commitment of members to the group (L_g), it is ready to proceed with the definition of the resources and skills that are required for the work (A_1). So the group moves from one major phase to the next. Once the G phase has been reached there could be several instances of different tasks (such as, G_1, G_2, G_3) without any basic reorganization in the group. In the case of the raft *Acali,* the first G was to cross the Atlantic ocean and reach Barbados. There the raft was refurbished and a decision made to continue through the Caribbean Ocean to Cozumel. The crew was now experienced, but the advent of the hurricane season created additional problems. The second part of the trip was seen by crew members as a distinct task, or a second G.

Whether the task is to conduct an ocean expedition, take part in a university course, or join any new group, some people drop out at different stages and some try to reorganize the group. The drop-outs are most likely to occur as the group moves from the subphases of "i" to "g" during the first two phases of L and A. In the first phase there are some persons who are attracted by the overall idea of the group but find that as the definition of the task is worked out in more detail, the group is not what they had in mind. Having developed relatively little commitment to the group at this stage, they drop out. Or, as in the case of the selection of crew members for the *Acali,* it is decided that they really do not fit in and are encouraged to leave.

Some persons may be satisfied with the purpose of the group but find that they are not satisfied when it is clear what the resources will be at the end of the A phase. They decide that there is not enough money to carry out the task as it was originally envisaged, or that the skill level in the group is not high enough, or that in some other way the group lacks resources. Although these persons have more invested in the group by this time, they may decide to drop out. If the members are satisfied with the level of resources they may stay on board until it becomes clear what the role distribution will be. Then they may discover that their own projected role is not satisfactory or that someone else seems to be taking over too much of the leadership function. At this point the dissatisfied members are more likely to decide to try to change the role relationships than they are to drop out. If they fail to make a move, there is nothing left but to carry out the task with the resources available and the roles as they have been designated. Since there must have been a majority of members or a minority of powerful members who have approved of the role definitions as they were developed, the work of reorganizing the group will be met with resistance. Hence the major conflict, or what in another context has been termed "the revolution within the revolution," is most likely to occur at this point in the group's development. For the *Acali,* this conflict came to a head as the raft was being towed out to sea to begin the expedition. However the "mutiny" was contained and the raft commenced its voyage, but not without further problems of role definition, some of which will be described as examples of role conflict in Chapter 8.

The terminal stage for some groups may not be clear-cut; groups may not die dramatically, but only fade away. However in the case of the *Acali,* the events were dramatic up to the very end. Bypassing all the histrionics that took place at Cozumel and Mexico City, a simplified version of the terminal stage for the *Acali* crew would center on the idea that they were no longer the *Acali* "family" but would return to their statuses as separate individuals in different parts of the world (L_1). For the purpose of the "debriefing," the group was isolated in a set of tourist lodges that had been rented for the occasion on Cozumel, complete with police guards to make sure that no unauthorized persons went in or out during the first week (L_a) and a professional staff of psychiatrists to conduct group and individual sessions with the crew members (L_i). The actual work of the terminal stage (L_g) included a series of confrontations between various subgroups of the crew and between some crew members and Genovés. Even "mother nature" seemed to be joining in the upheaval since we experienced an earthquake during the second phase of the terminal stage that was held in Mexico City. However, eventually the crew members did board their planes and return to their everyday lives. Genovés (1979) has given his version of the exercise in full-color books in Spanish and English.[2]

A Further Elaboration of the Phases

Thus far, the analysis of group development focuses primarily on the task side of the group through the content categories of AGIL. Since one of the "tasks" of a group is to develop an appropriate structure for each phase of its activity, this method of analysis combines some of the behaviors that others, Tuckman for example, divide into "group structure" and "task activity." With regard to the two types of "process" categories described in Chapter 1, we would expect that the categories for "task behavior" (Observe, hypothesize, propose action) would appear at approximately the same rate throughout the life of the group as each functional problem is taken up in turn. With regard to the "social-emotional" process categories (dominant-submissive, positive-negative, and so on), the relationship with the LAIG phases has already been indicated in Chapter 2. During the L phase the conforming-nonconforming dimension would be most salient, during the A phase, serious-expressive, during the I phase, positive-negative, and during the G phase, dominant-submissive.

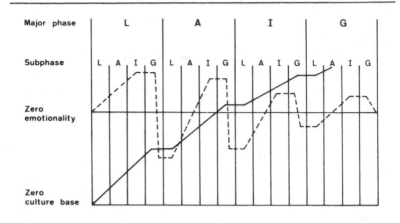

Figure 5.2 Relationship between Phases and Subphases of LAIG, Accumulation of
Group Culture, and Emotionality

It is now possible to combine the hypotheses concerning phases within phases with Shambaugh's generalizations concerning the accumulation of group culture and the oscillation between positive and negative feelings in the emotional area, as in Figure 5.2.

Moving from the top to the bottom of Figure 5.2, the first row of letters gives the indications of the limits of the major phases in the order L-A-I-G. For any actual group the phases will probably not be of the same length, and as indicated earlier, a group may recycle through a phase or not proceed beyond a given phase; however, only the simplest model is given here. The second row of letters indicates the subphases.

Next is a line showing the "zero" level of emotionality. When the graph is above the line, the emotions are positive; when it is below the line, the emotions are negative. Given the previous analysis of group development, positive feelings should reach a peak during each "i" subphase. Then positive feelings would fall off during the "g" subphase as the application of dominance (leadership) in the interest of the task either generates hard feelings or alternatively turns the group from a concern about interpersonal relationships. The low point of positive feeling might be expected to continue into the next subphase of "l" (in the next major phase) but for different reasons. As the group members begin the task of defining "the meaning of all this" for the particular subphase, they will probably discover that subgroups within the group have different ideas, and until the unity in the group has been restored, negative feelings will be evident as subgroups defend their different points of view. This is probably where Bales has observed the greatest degree of "polarization" in his "self-analytic" groups, with the greatest degree of "unification" occurring during the "i" subphase. Thus, if one disregards the task content and focuses with Shambaugh on positive and negative feelings or with Bales on changes in group structure, one will observe a continual oscillation.

The bottom line in Figure 5.2 gives the "zero" level of culture for the group. As in Shambaugh's analysis, culture "builds" during the positive emotional periods and shows no growth during the negative periods. But now the categories for content (AGIL) give an additional insight into the process, since it is primarily during the l,a, and i subphases that new points of view, understandings, practices, and norms are developed. During the g subphase the various resources (a) and norms (i) are used to carry out the task in line with the values agreed on at the beginning of the phase (1). We would not, therefore, expect much of an increment to the culture during the g subphase nor during the first part of the following l subphase while group members are still in disagreement over the overall guidelines for the next phase.

As further examples of the use of the AGIL categories in the analysis of group development, this chapter concludes with two case studies, the first a workshop on nonviolent action held in the United States (Hare, 1972: 360-363) and the second an institute for social science on the island of Curacao, Netherlands Antilles (Hare and Blumberg, 1977: 220-237, 281-282).

A Workshop on Nonviolent Action

As an example of the analysis of group development we can follow the events in a workshop on nonviolence held by the Friends Peace Committee of Philadelphia on a weekend in February 1970. The workshop was held at a Quaker meetinghouse in the suburbs. In all, 35 persons were present, about equally divided by sex, with an average age of 26 years (range 14 to 60). The majority had a college education. Although all participants were given personality tests and rated by several judges on the four interaction process dimensions, the major findings result from an analysis using the four functional categories (AGIL).

As the workshop progressed from Friday night through Saturday afternoon, it was possible to identify typical stages in group development. The workshop turned out to be successful because the trainers and members were able to deal with the basic functional problems faced by any group in the order that is most effective for learning groups.

Group Development During the
Workshop

Before the analysis of group development begins, the life of the group is divided into natural time periods. The duration of these time periods depends upon the length of time the group is in existence. In the Friends Peace Committee Workshop, the days provide the major breaks in activity and within each day the morning, afternoon, and evening sessions. If more detailed records of each session had been kept, the units might have been based on each change of activity, since each session included several different activities. However, in this case, the major trends of development are evident when the session is used as a unit. The sessions were: (1) Friday night, (2) Saturday morning, (3) Saturday afternoon, (4) Saturday evening, (5) Sunday morning, and (6) Sunday noon.

On Friday night some of the L or pattern-maintenance functions were performed as group members were registered, names and brief backgrounds given, and the trainers made an opening statement about the purpose of the workshop. Some orientation had been provided by the registration and announcement forms sent out prior to the workshop. Much of the definition of the basic goal of the workshop was given through actual participation in role-playing or other skill groups. The basic message was that the workshop would concentrate on skills rather than on philosophy or tactics of nonviolence. This definition was challenged by some group members who thought that there should be more emphasis on philosophy or a greater self-awareness in dealing with skills.

Actually it is possible to identify subphases within each of the major phases. In the L phase, for example, the subphases are L_1, L_a, L_i, and L_g. That is, in order to establish the general meaning of the workshop, the "big idea" is introduced by one or two individuals (L_1 or L sub 1); next, information is given or resources collected which will help to implement the idea (L_a); next, the group is organized to endorse the idea (L_i); and finally the idea is agreed upon (L_g).

On Friday night the main idea of the workshop was presented by the trainers (L_1). The idea was tested through actual role plays so that information could be gathered about the feasibility of the approach (L_a). The trainers indicated that they were "loose" and would entertain suggestions for sessions other than the ones originally proposed, thus bringing all the group members into the L process (L_i). Finally a definition of the workshop was fashioned which included new as well as old ideas (L_g).

We can guess that there must have been a similar set of pre-group subphases in the L sector when the Friends Peace Committee members met to outline their ideas about the workshop before they issued a call for participants. Here we see that many levels of analysis are possible. When we begin the workshop in the L phase, we are taking the point of view of the participants. From the trainers' viewpoint, this is the *work* which they planned to do some time before, and therefore represents the G phase for them.

Friday night's session was effective as an L stage because it allowed for a modification of the overall plan to meet the needs and skills of the particular set of participants who attended. This tended to give a higher degree of commitment to the program than any formulation which is simply laid on by someone in authority.

Saturday morning was primarily in the A sector as participants learned a variety of new skills. Saturday afternoon continued in A with two groups working on street speaking and guerrilla theater. When the group left the site of the workshop and drove into town to speak and perform in front of a supermarket, the group might seem to have moved into the G sector since they were actually doing the *work* they had come for. However, this was still in A since the group was not yet reorganized for the new task. The trainers were still in control. They had made all the arrangements and were directing the sessions. This is the point where classroom education usually stops. The teacher gives the students skills and perhaps tries them out on practice problems, but the students never act independently.

The move toward independence from the trainers began Saturday night, a traditional time for integrative (I) activity. The following morning one of the participants remarked that the singing the night before had given the group "soul." Group members now felt "together" enough to do something on their own.

The opportunity for independent action was provided Sunday morning when the trainer asked for volunteers to prepare a presentation for the Forum of the Friends Meeting whose facilities were being used. A group of participants took over this activity, planned it according to principles learned in the workshop, incorporated techniques and skills already learned, and produced an outstanding performance. Thus the group moved into the G sector, using their own resources.

We note that the participants who took the lead in this activity had shown their strength early in the workshop by volunteering to lead special sessions. A group composed of persons with less experience than the trainers who were the participants in this workshop might not have been able to "take over" as readily. Most teachers never give their students a chance. The student is put firmly in his place as "student" throughout the learning experience and never given an opportunity to use the new skills with his former teacher as resource person, co-participant, or subordinate.

The group passed again into the L stage during the evaluation at noon on Sunday. Here members summed up their experiences, prepared to sever their relationships with the workshop, and began to shift their commitment to the groups and tasks they had left behind.

In sum, the group passed through the expected stages of group development from L to A to I to G and back to L again. However, the trainers seemed to have placed their main emphasis on the L and A stages. The singing and integrative events which highlighted the I stage seem to have occurred because of the day of the week (Saturday night) and were more casually organized.

The Antillean Institute of Social Science

The Antillean Institute of Social Science was held on the island of Curacao, Netherlands Antilles, during June, July, and August of 1970. The Institute had been designed as an approach to nonviolent planned change using a community self-study as one response to the violent change that had occurred on the island on May 30, 1969 when rioting workers burned and looted the central business section of the town of Willemstad, after which the government of the Netherlands Antilles resigned (Hare, Carney, and Ovsiew, 1977).

Members of the business community of Curacao were accustomed to seeking expert advice to solve management problems or to introduce new manufacturing or marketing techniques. Thus when a major social problem erupted on the island, it was not surprising to find these same people turning once more to outsiders for advice. One group from the Chamber of Commerce had read about McClelland's methods for increasing "achievement motivation" and thought that a program of that type might be useful. It was (see Berlew and LeClere, 1974). From the Lions Club, the chairman, Victor Pinedo, Jr., wrote to an acquaintance in the United States asking for "someone to make a study of the situation and advise the community as to what action they should take to remedy the problem." Since I had had some experience that might prove relevant, Pinedo's letter was passed to me.

In an exchange of letters I suggested that one week be devoted to a preliminary survey of the problems of Curacao as a basis for a proposal for research or action. During the first two days of the week I asked that we meet some of the people who would be important to enable us to carry out any proposal we would formulate. We should also meet some of the people who would be potentially members of the research/ action team. Finally we should interview a set of persons representing a cross-section of those who had been actively involved in the recent events or who had been affected by them. By mid-week we would draw up a plan and then modify the plan and determine possible interest in it during the remaining days of the week.

As it turned out, each of the three one-week periods that were devoted to planning and the final ten-week period during which two sessions of the Institute were held represented one of the phases in the expected sequence of group development. The activities of the first phase were concentrated in one week of November 1969 when Pinedo and I developed the basic plan (L). The second phase reached a high point when I returned to the island in January with several colleagues to begin a major fundraising drive for the $60,000 that we had budgeted for the Institute (A). The third phase was again concentrated in a week in May when we recruited staff and worked out the details of the teaching and research activities (I). The final phase consisted of actually holding the sessions of the Institute (G).

For a more detailed analysis we can identify four phases within each of the major phases. Thus for the first phase of L we have the subphases of:

L_1 = Pinedo proposes action research.
L_a = Funds are raised for a fact-finding visit.
L_i = Pinedo and I find a small group of Curacaons who are interested in the idea of the Institute.
L_g = The broad outlines of the Institute are developed.

In a similar way the fundraising venture required an idea, some "seed" money for brochures and other publicity materials, a fundraising team, and the work of fundraising. The same fourfold processes continued through the I and G phases.

Although some people dropped out during the first two phases, a major confrontation was not faced until near the end of the third one-week visit to the island (I phase). A concern was expressed that the Institute staff was being dominated by the group of American specialists that I had recruited to supplement the personnel available on Curacao. In response, we cut down on the number of courses to be taught by Americans, told a few additional Americans who were potential staff members that we could not use them, and did not use family members of the American staff as part of the paid American team. I also offered to step down as Co-director to become the liaison with the American staff. My offer was not accepted. Since I did not hear about the final outcome of the deliberations of the Institute Board (composed of persons on Curacao) until after I had returned to the United States, I left the island the third time on an anxious note. It was possible that the "revolution within the revolution" might bring the plans for the Institute to a halt. It was little consolation to have a theory that a revolt against the leadership typically takes place in the third phase in groups of many types. However, the show did go on and a successful Institute was held.

Summary

Three theories of group development were reviewed in some detail as examples of the literature. Tuckman presented the first major review in 1965 based mainly on studies of therapy groups. He identified four phases each of which has two aspects: group structure and task behavior. For group structure the phases are: (1) testing and dependence, (2) intragroup conflict, (3) development of group cohesion, and (4) functional role-relatedness. For task behavior the phases are: (1) orientation and testing, (2) emotional response to task demands, (3) discussing oneself and other group members, and (4) emergence of insight. Later he added a fifth, terminal stage.

Mann (1967) was primarily concerned with the way members of a training group relate to the leader. He also identified five phases that he characterized as (1) initial complaining, (2) premature enactment, (3) confrontation, (4) internalization, and (5) separation and terminal review. Shambaugh (1978), drawing on experience with therapy groups, also distinguished two aspects of behavior in groups: emotionality and task activity. Emotionality is evident in a series of oscillations of feelings of closeness and separateness. Task activity is marked by increases in group culture. The culture building takes place mainly during the periods of positive feeling and closeness.

A functional theory of group development, suggested by Effrat, incorporates the essentials of each of these and other theories in a four phase sequence of L-A-I-G with a terminal phase of L. First the purpose of the group must be defined and the commitment of members secured (L), then resources and skills must be provided or acquired (A), next roles must be developed and a sufficiently high level of morale achieved (I), and then the group is ready to work on the task with the coordination of leadership (G). At the end of the group's life there is a terminal phase in which the group returns to L to redefine the relationships between members as the group is disbanded.

In a more elaborate version of the L-A-I-G sequence, one can observe the same sequence of phases within each of the major phases. Some persons may drop out of the group as it nears the completion of the first two phases of L and A. However the "revolution within the revolution" is most likely to occur near the end of the I phase if some members are dissatisfied with the leadership or the role distribution since by this time they have become committed to the idea of the group and the resources are adequate. If change does not occur at this point there is nothing left to do but to carry on the work.

Various levels of functional analysis were illustrated with examples from the voyage of the raft *Acali* across the Atlantic Ocean, a workshop for trainers in nonviolent action in the United States, and the development of a social science institute on the island of Curacao, Netherlands Antilles.

Notes

1. Cottle also uses the AGIL categories, but as they were originally defined by Parsons. Although the sequence of development that he records appears to be different because of the different use of the terms, it actually includes the same sequence given in the present analysis.

2. Following Schutz (1958) I had suggested in a previous example (Hare and Blumberg, 1977: 282) that the terminal phases for a group might be in the reverse order from that in which the group develops. This is probably still true in a larger sense, in that there may be more than one aspect to a terminal phase (such as giving up roles or redistributing funds). However the present version of the theory is probably most likely when a group consciously disbands.

Chapter 6
Social Control

Social control is the process by which an individual manipulates the behavior of others or by which group members bring pressure to bear on an individual. Social control can be *formal,* as represented by the rules and regulations enforced by persons in authority in a large organization, or it can be *informal,* as in the social pressure of members in a small intimate group. Although there are many cases where social control is applied forcibly by others, in most cases social control is *self-control.* This is the self-control that takes place during the initial phase of a social act when the individual modifies intended behavior as a result of the anticipated response of the other person. If the individual is at all effective in social relationships, the process of social control will be over before the overt act.

In the literature on small groups, the greatest interest in this subject has been shown in the experiments explicitly designed to demonstrate aspects of individual *conformity* to group norms. These include the classic studies of Sherif (1935), Asch (1955), and Milgram (1963). However, the same processes of control are evident in studies that deal with other aspects of social behavior, since individuals cannot act in concert without some form of conformity to norms. Thus, the literature on *leadership* describes the

AUTHOR'S NOTE: Various sections of this chapter are reprinted with permission of Macmillan Publishing Co., Inc. from *Handbook of Small Group Research* by A. Paul Hare. Copyright,© 1976 by The Free Press, a Division of Macmillan Publishing Co., Inc.—"Asch's Experiment on Judging Line Lengths," from pp. 21-23, 31-32; "Milgram's Shocking Experiment," from pp. 40-41; "A Functional Interpretation of Pressures to Conform," from pp.54-57.

The section on the role-playing experiment (including Tables 6.2, 6.3, and 6.4) was taken from A. P. Hare, H. M. Kritzer, and H. H. Blumberg, "Functional Analysis of Persuasive Interaction in a Role-Playing Experiment," *Journal of Social Psychology,* 107 (1979): 77-88. Copyright © Journal Press. Reprinted by permission.

control exerted by members who have high status in groups, while the literature on social *power* describes the controlling behavior of the ordinary member. Whether the social-psychologist sets out to study the "risky-shift," "helping behavior," "cooperation," or some other social-psychological process, it is soon apparent that some set of norms and some process of conformity is involved and a set of variables similar to those introduced in the Asch experiments is rediscovered.

As examples of research and theory on *conformity,* the experiments of Asch and Milgram will be summarized, followed by the theories proposed by Jahoda (1956) and Kelman (1958). Each of these experiments and theories will be related to a functional interpretation of pressures toward conformity. The functional approach is illustrated with data from a role-playing experiment.

Asch's Experiment on Judging Line Lengths

Solomon Asch, a psychologist of the Gestalt tradition, designed an ingenious study to yield objective measures of conformity of an individual's psycho-physical judgments when confronted by an incorrect majority opinion (Asch, 1955).

In this experiment, a number of persons are instructed by the experimenter to unanimously give incorrect judgments in what is ostensibly an experiment in visual perception. The stimulus materials are two sets of white cards. One set consists of cards, each of which displays a single black line (the standard). Each card of the other set bears three lines, one being the same length as the standard, the other two being easily recognizable departures from this length. These cards are illustrated in Figure 6.1. The task is to match the correct line of the three with the standard. All judgments are expressed orally. In the experiment proper, a single "naive" subject is placed in a group of "coached subjects," the total number varying in different experiments from seven to nine. The behavior of the "coached subjects" and the manner of assembling for the experiment give no indication of the collusion between group and experimenter. The naive subject is seated at the end (or in some cases next to the end) of the line of subjects. The experimenter shows a pair of cards and one by one the subjects state their opinions of the line which matches the standard. A series of eighteen trials consists of twelve critical trials, in which the coached members unanimously give incorrect responses, and six neutral trials, in which the coached members give correct responses. The performance in the experimental groups may be compared with a control series in which all members of the group are "naive" and uninstructed and merely write their judgments down on paper, trial by trial.

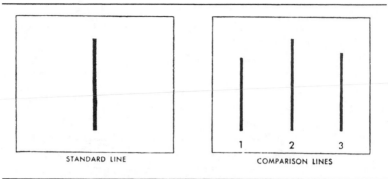

STANDARD LINE   COMPARISON LINES

Figure 6.1 A Pair of Stimulus Cards
SOURCE: Solomon E. Asch, "Opinions and Social Pressure," *Scientific American* 193 (November 1955): 35. Copyright © 1955 by Scientific American, Inc. All rights reserved. Reprinted by permission of the author and W. H. Freeman & Co.

Using this basic experimental design, 123 college students were placed in the minority situation described above. When a subject was faced with an incorrect majority opinion, there was a significant increase in his errors, always in the direction of the majority. Nearly 37 percent of the subjects' responses were in error, as compared with almost no error in the control groups. Thus, influence of group opinion on individuals was in many cases sufficient to dissuade them from responding in terms of his immediate sense impressions, which were clearly in contradiction to the group. However, in most instances a different judgment by the majority was not enough to make the individual conform.

The percentage of the 123 subjects who made correct judgments on each of the twelve critical trials is indicated in Figure 6.2, by a solid line. The accuracy of subjects who are not under group pressure is indicated by a dotted line. The largest percentage of correct judgments was made on the first critical trial (over 80 percent), while the smallest percentage of correct judgments was made on the fourth trial (less than 50 percent).

More information about the subjects who yielded and those who did not was obtained in the interviews which were conducted with the subjects immediately after the experiment. Asch interpreted his interviews as indicating three types of independent subjects and three types of yielding subjects. Among independent subjects he found independence accompanied by confidence. This type of individual was aware of majority opinion, but did not allow it to shake reliance on the evidence. A different type was the withdrawn individual, who seemed to be more oriented in terms of "explicit principles concerning the necessity of being an individual." His third type was described as independent, but felt anxious and

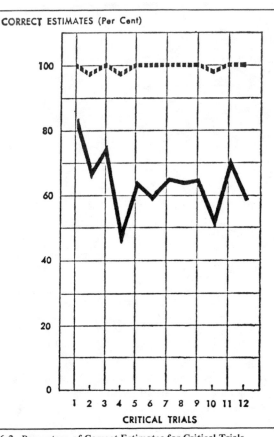

Figure 6.2 **Percentage of Correct Estimates for Critical Trials**

SOURCE: Solomon E. Asch, "Opinions and Social Pressure," *Scientific American* 193 (November 1955): 35. Copyright © 1955 by Scientific American, Inc. All rights reserved. Reprinted by permission of the author and W. H. Freeman & Co.

uncomfortable over the public declaration of minority judgments. This individual would rather be with the majority but was unwilling to join them at the cost of discarding sensory impressions, which were in this instance so clear.

The subjects who yielded on more than half of the critical trials were categorized by Asch into those who distorted their perception, those who distorted their judgment (decided they were inaccurate and the group was accurate), and those who distorted their action, yielding overtly only because of a great need not to appear deviant in the group.

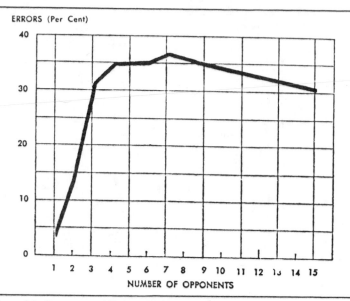

Figure 6.3 **Percentage of Errors with Majorities of One to Fifteen Opponents**
SOURCE: Solomon E. Asch, "Opinions and Social Pressure," *Scientific American*
193 (November 1955): 35. Copyright © 1955 by Scientific American, Inc. All rights
reserved. Reprinted by permission of the author and W. H. Freeman & Co.

In a variation of the same experiment the naive subject was given a
"partner" who gave the true estimate of the line length. The effect of this
alliance was to reduce the number of times that the subject would
conform with the majority. However, if the partner changed over to the
majority opinion in the middle of the experiment, the majority's influence
was again felt with full force. On the other hand, if the partner began with
the majority and joined the naive subject halfway through the experiment,
the subject was encouraged to become independent of the majority.

In one series Asch varied the size of the opposition from one to fifteen
persons. The results, which are given in Figure 6.3, showed a clear trend.
When a subject was confronted by a single individual who contradicted his
answers, he continued to answer independently and correctly on nearly all
trials. When the opposition was increased to two, the pressure became
substantial. Minority subjects now accepted the wrong answer 13.6 percent of the time. Under the pressure of a majority of three, the subjects'
errors jumped to 31.8 percent. However, further increases in the size of
the majority only increased the tendency to conform to majority opinion
by a relatively small percentage. Asch concluded that when naive subjects
were confronted with the contradictory opinion of only one or two

persons they remained relatively independent. But when three persons were in opposition, the full effect of the majority was felt and no further significant differences appeared with majorities as large as fifteen.

Milgram's Shocking Experiment

In 1963 Stanley Milgram published an article describing a procedure for the study of destructive obedience in the laboratory. He was motivated by the same concern that was shared by Sherif, Asch, Lewin, and the other social psychologists who had performed experiments on conformity 20 years earlier, at the time of World War II. Given that obedience is a basic element in the structure of social life and that some system of authority is a requirement for all communal living, how is it that the tendency to obey can override training in ethics, sympathy, and moral conduct? In particular, how was it possible for some persons in Germany in 1933-1945 to obey orders to kill millions of people?

Milgram devised a procedure for studying obedience which consisted of ordering a naive subject to administer electric shock to a victim. A simulated shock generator was used, with 30 clearly marked voltage levels that ranged from 15 to 450 volts. The instrument bore verbal designations that ranged from "Slight Shock" to "Danger: Severe Shock." The responses of the victim, who was a trained confederate of the experimenter, were standardized. The orders to administer shocks were given to the naive subject in the context of a "learning experiment" ostensibly set up to study the effects of punishment on memory. As the experiment proceeded, the naive subject was commanded to administer increasingly more intense shocks to the victim, even to the point of reaching the level marked "Danger: Severe Shock." Internal resistances became stronger, and at a certain point the subject refused to go on with the experiment. Behavior prior to this rupture was considered "obedience," in that the subject complied with the commands of the experimenter. The point of rupture was the act of disobedience. A quantitative value was assigned to the subject's performance based on the maximum intensity shock he was willing to administer before he refused to participate further. Thus for any particular subject and for any particular experimental condition the degree of obedience was specified with a numerical value. The crux of the study was to systematically vary the factors believed to alter the degree of obedience to the experimental commands.

The subjects were 40 males between the ages of 20 and 50. They answered a newspaper advertisement which led them to believe that they would participate in a study of memory and learning. A wide range of occupations was represented in the sample including postal clerks, high school teachers, salesmen, engineers, and laborers. They were paid $4.50 for their participation in the experiment.

Milgram had expected that no more than 3 percent of the subjects would conform to the experimenter's commands to administer more than a "very strong shock." Thus the actual results of his first experiment were also quite "shocking" to him. He found that with few exceptions the subjects were convinced of the reality of the situation. During the experiment many subjects showed signs of extreme tension including sweating, trembling, groaning, and having fits of laughter.

Upon the command of the experimenter all of the 40 subjects went beyond the expected break-off point. Five refused to go beyond the 300-volt level, four gave one further shock, and five gave between 330 and 375 volts. Thus Milgram notes that 14 subjects "defied" the experimenter. From a tape recording, the comments of one of the subjects are given at the point where he broke off:

[Subject A] I think he's trying to communicate, he's knocking. . . .
Well it's not fair to shock the guy . . . these are terrific volts. I don't
think this is very humane. Oh I can't go on with this. No, this isn't
right. It's a hell of an experiment. The guy is suffering in there. No, I
don't want to go on. This is crazy.

Of the subjects, 26 obeyed the orders of the experimenter until the end, although they often did so under extreme stress. Some expressed fears similar to those who defied the experimenter, yet they obeyed.

After the maximum shocks had been delivered by the 26 subjects and the experimenter called a halt to the experiment, many obedient subjects heaved sighs of relief, mopped their brows, or showed other signs of relief, although some remained calm throughout.

The experiments of Asch and Milgram set off waves of replications and variations, generally with comparable results.

A Functional Interpretation of Pressures to Conform

In the mid-1950s both Jahoda (1956) and Kelman (1958) outlined theories of conformity which illustrate an application of the cybernetic hierarchy of control in functional theory, although neither seemed to be aware of the similarity at the time. Johoda's paper provides an example of four types of conformity which turn out to match A,G,I, and L.*

*From M. Jahoda, "Psychological Issues in Civil Liberties," *American Psychologist* 11 (1956): 233-237. Copyright © 1956 by the American Psychological Association. Reprinted by permission.

At the time of Jahoda's research, civil liberties, especially centering on the loyalty oath, were a dominant issue in universities in the United States. Although Jahoda had conducted several surveys about this issue, she does not cite her own research evidence, but rather makes up an incident which she feels illustrates all the processes of conformity which are involved. Jahoda (1956: 236) notes that any similarity with actual events is purely coincidental.

A college president together with a faculty committee of four persons considers applicants for a new appointment. The best qualified man is one who is known to be a socialist. Each of the four faculty members initially favors his appointment. The president recommends rejection because of the candidate's unsuitable political views. He adds that such an appointment would furthermore seriously offend a benefactor of the college who is about to make a substantial gift to it. As it happens, in this fictitious example, all four members of the faculty go along with the president's recommendation and reject the candidate.

Since each of the faculty members went along with the president's recommendation, we might suppose that they were all equally conforming. However, Jahoda (1956: 233-237) suggests that we use our imagination to hold confidential conversations with each of them after the event. They turn out to have four different stories:

Faculty member A says: "I feel awful. I still believe that we should not have considered the candidate's political views. But I couldn't stand up to the President. I admit I acted out of fear. The question of my promotion will come up next week."

Faculty member B says: "We had an interesting meeting. Originally I was quite opposed to the notion of considering a candidate's political views. But I changed my mind. The President made a very good argument against the inappropriateness of socialism for our country. He really convinced me of the mistake of deliberately exposing our students to an unrealistic idealist."

Faculty member C says: "I go to these meetings solely because I have been appointed to the committee. I really am not very much interested in these matters. But it is nice to sit together with the President and my colleagues. It makes me feel good to have close friendly contact with them. And if a group of nice people agree, I am the last to make difficulties. I think we did the right thing today."

Faculty member D says: "This was a really difficult decision for me. I still believe in academic freedom. But the argument that convinced

	Belief changed	Belief unchanged
Argument	Consentience L (Faculty member B)	Convergence A (Faculty member D)
Pressure (unrelated to issue)	Conformance I (Faculty member C)	Compliance G (Faculty member A)

Figure 6.4 Four Processes of Conformism
SOURCE: Marie Jahoda, "Psychological Issues in Civil Liberties," *American Psychologist* 11 (1956): 236. Copyright 1956 by the American Psychological Association. Reprinted by permission of the publisher.

> me was that I know the college depends on getting that gift. After all you can fight for academic freedom only if you have a college that can pay its expenses. I decided to reject the candidate because the President was right when he said we would never get that gift otherwise."

Jahoda then suggests that these four types can be explained by two underlying dimensions: first, whether the subject was moved by the argument or by pressure, and second, whether his belief was changed or unchanged as a result. This cross-classification is presented in Figure 6.4.

The four types fit the AGIL scheme directly as we rotate Figure 6.4 counter-clockwise one position: the process of convergence is related to adaptation (A) since it is based on facts, compliance to goal attainment (G) since it is based on the power of an authority, conformance to integration (I) since it is based on friendship ties, and consentience to pattern maintenance (L) since it is based on adherence to basic values. Following the cybernetic hierarchy of control we would expect conformity pressures of type L to be the most powerful, then I, then G, and last of all A.

Although Jahoda does not discuss these types in connection with the cybernetic hierarchy of control, her further examples and illustrations suggest reasons why the hierarchy of control might function as it does. Let us consider what it would take to change the minds of the four faculty members after their meeting with the president. The person who was convinced by the facts (A) should be the easiest to influence. Give him a new set of facts and he should reach a different decision. Next would come the person who complied through threat of loss of promotion (G). If he was actually promoted, or if in some other way the threat could be removed, he should be free to change. More difficult to change would be the person who enjoyed being with a friendly group (I). Even in another situation, this group might remain as a positive reference group and provide an anchorage for his opinions. If he were placed in a new group, the new group would have to appear more salient to him if he were to change. Finally the most difficult to change would be the person who has actually taken over the beliefs of the president (L). Since he now considers the beliefs his, it becomes a matter of his own integrity to maintain them.

Kelman (1958) identified only three processes, which he called compliance (G), identification (I), and internalization (L). A separate "A" process was not described. He defines his processes in terms similar to Jahoda's. He then continues by offering some hypotheses concerning the conditions under which each type of behavior is performed. The hypotheses are as follows:

(1) When an individual adopts an induced response through compliance, he tends to perform it only under conditions of surveillance by the influencing agent.
(2) When an individual adopts an induced response through identification, he tends to perform it only under conditions of salience of his relationship to the agent.
(3) When an individual adopts an induced response through internalization, he tends to perform it under conditions of relevance of the issue, regardless of surveillance or salience.

These propositions of Kelman's add something to our understanding of how the cybernetic hierarchy of control actually works. It is not that information is more controlling than energy in some abstract way, but that the information, in the form of values, is carried within the individual while the factors which depend on energy are external. Beginning at the top, the values (L) are the most powerful, since once they are internalized, the individual carries them with him. Next come the norms representing reciprocal role relationships (I). Once adopted through identification, they can be called up whenever the other person is present or whenever the relationship is "salient" for some other reason. Next in order comes the response to the power of a task supervisor (G), since it will only be effective while the supervisor is present. Last would be the power of money or another energy source as a means of influence in the adaptive area. Although Kelman does not include this type of influence in his experiment, it should have the least power because money only insures a response at the moment it is exchanged. Once the deal is closed, the vote is purchased, or whatever form of influence was sought is obtained, the money has no continuing influence. For the next round, more money must be produced if the influence is to be maintained. In a similar way, other sources of high energy tend to be consumed in use.

Unfortunately few experiments consider more than one variable at a time, so that it is difficult to find evidence to support the hypothesis that four types of influence on conformity are ordered according to the L,I,G,A hierarchy. Kelman's (1958) experiment demonstrates that variables of the L,I, and G types have an influence on attitude change (see also Leet-Pellegrini and Rubin, 1974), and experiments by Kiesler and colleagues give evidence that commitment to continue in a group (L) is a more powerful influence on conformity than attraction to the group (I) (Kiesler and Corbin, 1965; Kiesler, Zanna, and deSalvo, 1966; Kiesler, 1969, 1971).

Asch's experiment (1955) on judging lengths of lines provide the best illustration of the cybernetic hierarchy. He showed that individuals could be influenced by a coached majority giving incorrect answers, but that this effect would be countered by having at least one person agree with the subject. Further, the majority would have some influence no matter how extreme its opinion appeared to be. However, over 60 percent of the subjects held out against the majority. Many of these subjects said that they typically held out for their own opinions or that they considered the judgments an individual task. These results illustrate the hypothesis that a variable related to pattern maintenance (defining the task as one of individual judgment) was more powerful than an integrative variable (having a partner). The integrative variable was in turn more powerful than a goal-attainment variable (majority pressure). Finally, the adaptive variable (modifying the length of the line) was the least powerful.

The results of the Milgram experiments were similar. Although the effect of the shocks was unambiguous (A), the authority of the experimenter was much more powerful as an influence (G). This power could in turn be modified if one other subject appeared to defy the experimenter (I). Finally, the value the subject placed on not harming another human was the most effective deterrent (L).

Persuasive Interaction in a Roleplaying Experiment

To provide some evidence for the relative importance of L, I, G, and A variables in social conformity, Hare, Kritzer, and Blumberg (1979) conducted a role-playing experiment in which 186 male undergraduates were separately confronted by someone (an actor) asking them to sign a petition in a laboratory study of multifactorial design. Both the actor's behavior and the subject's response were rated using the categories for four-dimensional analysis, given in Chapter 2, and a version of the AGIL categories developed especially for the analysis of situations involving conformity (Hare, 1977: 277). These categories are given in Table 6.1 in the order of the cybernetic hierarchy of control with L at the top and A at the bottom. There are two sets. The first column indicates the behavior

TABLE 6.1   Functional Categorization of Conformity

Category	Behavior Characteristic of Person	
	Urging Conformity	Responding to Pressures to Conform
Pattern-maintenance (L)	Urges conformity on basis of common values (i.e, you are a good citizen); stresses commitment to issue.	Affirms or denies common value system.
Integration (I)	Urges conformity for sake of friendship. Person will be very pleased if other conforms. Cites positive value of belonging to a group of people who have conformed.	Shows concern for personal feelings of other. Cites a reference group that would support own opinion.
Goal-attainment (G)	Attempts to be coercive by personally bringing weight of opinion to bear on other; or by citing majority opinion, or opinion of someone who might be expected to have power over other.	Shows concern for majority opinion. Makes it clear that he or she is (or is not) a free agent in making decisions.
Adaptation (A)	Gives information as if facts will speak for themselves.	Asks for information or gives information on the issue.

SOURCE: A. P. Hare and H. H. Blumberg, *Liberation Without Violence* (London: Rex Collings, Ltd., 1977), p. 277. Reprinted by permission of the publisher.

characteristic of a person urging conformity and the second column a person responding to pressures to conform.

When one urges conformity on the basis of common values, or stresses commitment to issues, the behavior is coded L. Pressure for the sake of friendship or because some positive or negative reference group holds a given attitude is I. An attempt to coerce opinion change through leadership or majority opinion is coded as an instance of G. Finally, an attempt to urge conformity by offering money or by giving facts can be seen as an A pressure. In the second column, the person responding to pressures to conform is coded according to whether or not that person is open to each of these kinds of pressures.

Method

Students enrolled in Temple University summer school (N = 186) were recruited as subjects (Ss). For the interaction part of the experiment, S was ushered into a classroom through a door at the back. At the front of the classroom was a stage-set representing a grocer's shopfront. Seated at or standing near a small table outside of the grocer's was a man of student age (who was in reality a graduate student of drama). Also in the classroom was a videotape camera with operator and several graduate students who were observing and making ratings of the actors and Ss to provide additional tests of reliability for the ratings made by Hare and Blumberg which were used in the analysis below. S was told to assume that he was on his way to the grocer's, and that he would be asked something as he approached the shop. By using a role-playing experiment rather than observation under field conditions we expected, along with Willis and Willis (1970) to discover some of the larger, more obvious effects, but that some of the subtle effects might go undetected.

The first actor was used with all versions of the experimental variables (as described below—each combination occurred only once, in random sequence), and a second actor was used with a replication of a quarter of the total experiment (S as self, questionnaire before experiment). Both actors and all Ss were male. The number of Ss is greater than the number of experimental cells, because those conditions which, by random assignment, employed black Ss were replicated with white Ss in order to avoid confounding the experiment with an additional variable, race.

The actor engaged the S in a short conversation during which he tried to persuade S to sign a petition. The conversations lasted about a minute or a minute and a half, an amount of time comparable to that taken by petitioners in natural settings. The action was terminated when S signed or clearly indicated an intention not to sign. In each encounter the actor played a role which represented some combination of dominant or submissive, positive or negative, and serious or expressive behavior. For instance, as one of eight possibilities, the actor might have been asked to behave in a submissive-positive-serious manner. As a fourth variable, in the value area (L), the actor dressed in a "straight" fashion when he presented a petition opposed to an increase in social security benefits ("antiwelfare") and in a "hippie" fashion when he presented a "prowelfare" petition.

As three further experimental variables, the petitions either had no signatures or else about 10 signatures already on them (a variable in the G area [Blake, 1958; Phillips, 1972] S was asked either to be himself or to play a suburbanite (another variable in the value area [L]). Finally, the encounters took place either before or after a battery of psychological tests and other questionnaires were given to S, since the sequence could affect both the test scores and the behavior during the experiment (Kroger, 1968).

Various measures and questionnaires about demographic background and personality were administered to Ss, partly within a separate program of test development and partly as a test of the expectation that these individual differences would not interact with experimental variables.

All interaction was scored live by several observers with the use of the four-dimensional interaction-process category system. Later the interaction was scored again, from videotape, with the use of the same system in order to measure reliability and with the use of the scheme for functional (AGIL) analysis. Each S also filled out a postsession questionnaire.

It was only immediately before each encounter that the actor learned which "part" he was to play. He turned over a card which indicated some combination of the dominant, positive, and serious dimensions in random order. The observers did not know which condition was being run. The variations in types of petition and dress were "run in blocks."

Results and Discussion

Reliabilities for the two category systems for one pair of observers are given in Table 6.2. The coefficients are calculated from "single-judgment" data which would be expected to be less reliable than scores based on a number of averaged ratings. In general the reliabilities are higher for the actor, who spoke for a longer period of time, than for the S, who sometimes barely spoke at all. Reliabilities are also higher for the four-dimensional process system, on which the observers had had considerable practice, than for the AGIL scheme, which was being applied for the first time. The self-self reliabilities for one observer who used the four-dimensional categories both live and from videotape are higher than between-observer reliabilities.

Actor's Effect on S's Response

There were no significant correlations between actor and S on the dimensions of dominance-submission or on conforming-nonconforming. Postive behavior by the actor was significantly correlated (.32) with positive behavior by S. Also, there was a small but statistically significant correlation between serious behavior by the actor and serious behavior by S. These associations may be partly due to the raters' response sets (Blumberg, 1973).

Correlations between the four dimensions of observed behavior for the actors provided a test of how well the actors were playing their roles. Since

TABLE 6.2   Reliabilities of Categories

Dimension or area	Actor	Subject
Intercoder reliabilities for process of interaction[a]		
Dominance-submission	.61	.53
Positive-negative	.67	.36
Serious-expressive	.70	.45
Conforming-nonconforming	.53	.76
Intercoder reliabilities for content of interaction[b]		
Adaptation	.65	.57
Goal-attainment	.64	−.38
Integration	.34	.25
Latent pattern-maintenance	.56	.20
Intracoder reliabilities for process of interaction[c]		
Dominance-submission	.45	.76
Positive-negative	.69	.62
Serious-expressive	.84	.52
Conforming-nonconforming	.67	.70

[a]Correlations between scores for Hare and Blumberg for four dimensions of social interaction ($N = 184$).

[b]Correlations between scores for Hare and Blumberg for AGIL categories of pressures to conform.

[c]Correlations between scores for Blumberg coding live and from videotape for four dimensions of social interaction.

the actors were given the various combinations (as independent factors of dominant or submissive, positive or negative, and serious or expressive) in random order to enact as roles, there should have been no large correlations between these behaviors in the actual encounters. These correlations were close to zero and not significant. However, the actor's conforming-nonconforming behavior was left free to vary (rated "conformity" refers to the style of interaction, which would not necessarily correspond to the "conformity" manifest in the actor's style of dress and content of petition). As it turned out, when the actor was dominant and serious, he was also seen as conforming and urging conformity of the S, correlations of .24 and .42, respectively.

There was also a significant difference between the actors. One of them was much more positive when he was asked to be dominant. He would place his arm around S and in other ways show more overt friendliness.

Comparison of the Two Systems of Categories

Table 6.3 gives the correlations between the four-dimensional process categories and the AGIL system for the actors. We had expected that

TABLE 6.3   Relationships (r) Between Categories in Four Dimensions and AGIL Systems[a]

Dimension	Adaptation	Goal attainment	Integration	Latent pattern maintenance
Dominant	.25	.35	.06	.23
Positive	−.04	−.66	.38	−.03
Serious	.50	.13	−.19	.28
Conforming	.14	.15	−.15	.16

Note: For $N = 150$, a correlation of .16 is significant at the .05 level and .21 at the 0.1 level.

[a]Hare's ratings ($N = 185$).

dominant behavior would be most highly (positively) associated with Goal-attainment, positive behavior with Integration, serious with Adaptation, and conforming with Latent pattern maintenance and tension management. In the first three cases, the highest positive correlation between pairs of categories is located in the expected cell. For the fourth area, although conforming behavior is significantly correlated with pattern maintenance, the correlation is barely higher than it is between conformity and the other AGIL categories. Perhaps this is because conforming-nonconforming and pattern maintenance were the most difficult to score. Further there is a high negative correlation between the positive behavior of the actor and his persuasive attempts in the goal-attainment area. This simply means that when the actor was being coercive he was seen as quite negative.

Other Effects

Whether the battery of psychological tests was given before or after the roleplay made a significant difference (at the .05 level or better) in a number of instances. Comparing Ss who were given the tests before the roleplay encounter (N = 76) with those who were given the tests afterwards (N = 74), all with the same actor, we found that those taking the tests beforehand were lower in yea-saying, higher in verbal IQ, and more dominant and serious in the encounter. They took considerably less time in the encounter (73 seconds vs. 115 seconds). Also the actor was not as strong in his demands for conformity. This suggests that Ss who had already sat through up to an hour's testing were eager to finish the roleplay. They "came on" in a dominant, serious manner and finished in considerably less time. The actor, in turn, was less inclined to press them to conform. Since Ss had plenty of time for the psychological tests, they were less likely to give uncritical answers (yea-saying) and more likely to

TABLE 6.4   Mean Ratings of S Conformity by S Role, Petition Issue, and Dominance of Actor's Role

S role	Dominant		Submissive	
	Mean	N	Mean	N
Self				
Prowelfare	4.52	27	4.50	26
Antiwelfare	2.50	28	2.92	24
Suburbanite				
Prowelfare	2.38	21	3.27	22
Antiwelfare	4.35	20	3.82	17

Note: N = 185. F test significant at .04 level.

seek out the right answer on the IQ test. The number of signatures on the petition had no overall effect.

Effective Persuasion

The major findings of the experiment with regard to conditions found to affect the conforming behavior of S are illustrated in Table 6.4. The table gives the mean ratings for S's conformity (mainly, rating of the S's readiness to sign the petition) for various combinations of S's role (playing self or a suburbanite), the issue described in the petition (prowelfare or antiwelfare), and whether or not the actor was instructed to play a dominant or submissive role. The major effect is produced by the combination of S's role and the issue on the petition. When S was playing himself and the petition was prowelfare, conformity was quite likely, an indication that most Ss were in fact "prowelfare." However, when S was playing the suburbanite and when the petition was antiwelfare, conformity was most likely an indication that most Ss believe that suburbanites are antiwelfare.

Further, the highest conformity within each S role occurred when the actor was dominant and the petition was consistent with S's role. It appears that when the petition was consistent with S's role, increased dominance on the part of the actor was likely to lead to increased conformity on the part of S. However, if the petition was not in line with the values implied in the role, then an actor who "came on strong" was likely to "turn off" S and make conformity less likely. The conclusion would seem to be to use a "soft sell" on those whose values are dissimilar to yours and reserve the "hard sell" for your friends. A similar effect is reported by Nesbitt (1972) who tried to persuade community residents in the United States to take a position against the Vietnam war. A written pamphlet had no effect while an oral communication by a student had a negative effect. Presumably this also indicates that the community resident was "turned off" by pressure from a student with a different value position.

The results confirm the hypothesis that a factor which is related to values (pro- or antiwelfare) is more important in determining conformity than a factor which is related to goal attainment (interpersonal dominance).

In demonstrating that the content of a petition is generally more crucial than manner of presentation, our findings are similar to those of Konečni and Ebbesen (1975). They expected that—if a petitioner were a child or were accompanied by a child rather than being a lone adult—suburban women would be more likely to sign a petition "appropriate for children" and less likely to sign one that was "inappropriate for children." However, in an actual field test, only the overall difference between petitions had a significant effect.

In our experiment the correlation between the conformity of S and the positive behavior of the actor over all conditions was .20 (significant at the .01 level) compared with a correlation of .08 between S's conformity and the actor's dominance, and .07 between S's conformity and the actor's seriousness. This suggests that a variable related to integration is more important than one related to goal-attainment or adaptation.

To provide additional insight, several other analyses were performed, all with similar results. One applied ANOVA to the ratings of Ss' conformity as the dependent variable and five experimental dimensions as the independent variables. In the $2 \times 2 \times 2 \times 2 \times 2$ design, L was represented by either the content of the petition or the actor's dress, G by either the actor's programmed dominance or whether the petition presented to the S already had signatures on it, I by the actor's programmed positiveness, and A by the actor's programmed seriousness.

Separate analyses of variance were carried out for S playing himself and for S playing a suburbanite. For both analyses a large and significant main effect appeared for the L variable (in the directions noted above). Specifically, for S as self, the prowelfare petition was more likely to be signed ($p < .001$), as manifest in Hare's rating of conformity; and for S as suburbanite, antiwelfare signatures were more likely ($p < .001$). The only other significant main effects were due to I and G variables: the actor's positiveness, in the case of S as suburbanite ($p < .05$), both increased the likelihood of conformity (that is, signing the petition). For each analysis there was one significant interaction effect. The significant interaction brought additional "G" variables into the picture. In the case of S as self, it was the interaction among I and the two "G" variables ($p < .01$). Ss were especially likely to sign when the presentation was dominant-signatures (already present)-positive, and especially unlikely to sign in the condition of submissive-no signatures-negative. In the case of S as suburbanite, there was a significant L $\times$ G interaction: as discussed above, dominance led to increased signing of the antiwelfare petition and less signing of the prowelfare petition.

We can infer from the combination of the results of the correlations and the analyses of variance that the relative effect of the various pressures to conform is consistent with the expected order L-I-G-A, although the evidence is most conclusive for L in relation to the other variables.

Summary

Although social control can be exerted through formal rules or informal group pressure, in most cases self-control is sufficient to modify intended behavior before an act becomes overt. Social psychologists have been concerned with the process of conformity to norms since the beginning of the discipline, however the rise of Hitler in Germany in the 1930s and the devastating effects of his regime gave a renewed impetus to research. The studies by Asch, who asked naive subjects to judge the similarity of line lengths in the presence of coached majorities, and of Milgram, who commanded subjects to administer what they believed to be increasing electric shocks to another subject, are representative of the experimental work in this field. In both cases, some subjects gave in to pressure from the majority or from a person in authority. However, in each case some subjects refused to conform and the presence of other variables, such as having someone appear to support the naive subject, decreased the likelihood of conformity.

The theories of Jahoda and Kelman suggest reasons why different types of variables might have different effects. Their work can in turn be understood in terms of the four functional categories (AGIL) and the cybernetic hierarchy. For example, one can urge conformity on the basis of common values (L), for the sake of friendship (I), because a majority or someone in authority dominates the scene (G), or because of the facts of the case (A). From the cybernetic hierarchy one would expect L variables to be the most persuasive and A variables the least. Values (L) once internalized will be the hardest to change; next are norms (I) represented by reciprocal role relationships, which are effective as long as they are salient; next comes the power of the majority or an authority (G), which is effective only under conditions of surveillance; and last comes the influence of the facts or money (A), which is only effective at the time of the exchange.

A role-playing experiment in which subjects are asked to sign a petition by an actor who assumes different roles provided some support for the hypothesis concerning the relative importance of the L, I, G, and A variables. In this case the values represented by the petition have the most marked effect.

Chapter 7
Interpersonal Choice

As noted in Chapter 1, Moreno was largely responsible for introducing "sociometry" as a method of revealing interpersonal choices in groups. Moreno (1953) suggested six rules to be followed in using the "sociometric test":

(1) The limits of the group in which the test is given should be indicated.
(2) There should be unlimited choices of other persons.
(3) Individuals should be asked to choose and reject other group members with a specific criterion or activity in mind.
(4) The results of the sociometric test should be used to restructure the group; that is, the group should be reorganized by placing people together who have chosen each other as liked.
(5) The opinions should be given in private.
(6) Questions should be phrased in ways that members can understand.

In practice, Lindzey and Borgatta (1954) estimated that these six rules were followed in only about 25 percent of all sociometric studies. The most frequent deviations from the rules are the limitation on choices, usually to about three, and the omission of the action step of actually reorganzing the group in line with the results of the test. Some studies also omit a criterion such as "Whom would you choose to work with?" and ask

AUTHOR'S NOTE: The sections of this chapter on the sociogram, choice criteria, reciprocal choice, bases of friendship, and morale and cohesiveness are reproduced with few changes from A. Paul Hare, *Handbook of Small Group Research* (pp. 153-156, 163-166, 170-172). Copyright © 1976 by Macmillan Publishing Co., Inc. Reprinted with permission of Macmillan Publishing Co., Inc. (To make the text easier to follow, I have only included citations to the literature where a particular work is mentioned. The other citations may be found in the original text.)

only "Whom do you like?" This second type of question has been called "near sociometric."

Moreno was very serious about having a specific criterion and reorganizing the group or groups on the basis of the pattern of choices, since for him this was the whole point of the exercise. He wanted to recreate societies by placing people in mutually supportive groups. The only opportunity he had to try this out on any relatively large set of individuals was at a home for delinquent girls at Hudson, New York. There, with the help of Helen Jennings, he reorganized living and work groups on the basis of tests revealing interpersonal choices and on various role-playing tests for spontaneity. He appears to have made life happier for many of the girls and reduced the rate at which girls would run away from the institution (Moreno, 1953).

On occasion practical use has been made of the sociometric test, as in the American Army during World War II when groups of "buddies" were sent in as replacements for infantry units, thus reducing the casualty rate below that when men were sent as individuals from replacement depots to front line outfits. Or again when school "sociometricians" in the United States assigned elementary school children to reading groups on the basis of their sociometric choices. However, most of the research using sociometric tests has been with classrooms of university students or with ad hoc laboratory groups. Thus the typical summary of research on interpersonal attraction is only a pale reflection of what is happening in the real world (Byrne and Griffitt, 1973). Although some reviews stress field studies (Secord and Backman, 1964; Huston and Levinger, 1978), it is the anthropologists rather than the psychologists or sociologists who have provided most of the documentation of the importance of friendship in social systems.

In contrast to the limited role expectations that may be placed on the "best-liked" person in a laboratory group, the role of "friend" in the larger society is particularistic, personal, diffusely affective, fully institutionalized, and always instrumental in the economic sphere and sometimes more broadly (Ramsøy, 1968). Translating this last sentence from functional terminology, it means that a friend is someone you can count on to help out in providing for your economic well-being and probably across the board. For example, in one African tribe, a good friend, who lives some distance away, will keep your extra cattle for you so that your relatives will not know the size of your herd (Gulliver, 1972). In an urban setting, the gangs described by Whyte in *Street Corner Society* (1943) represent the type of friendship that provides the basic mode through which its members related to the larger society. Or, as Huston and Levinger (1978) have put it: "our deeper relationships do much to locate us in social and psychological space."

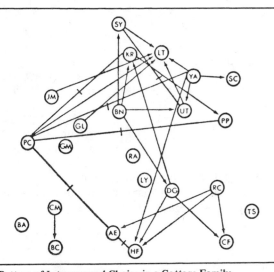

Figure 7.1 Pattern of Interpersonal Choice in a Cottage Family
SOURCE: Jacob L. Moreno, *Who Shall Survive?*, rev. ed. (Beacon, N.Y.: Beacon House, 1953), p. 267. Reprinted by permission of the publisher.

Generally, Moreno bypassed the issue of why people choose each other, except to notice who was "overchosen" and "underchosen" and to help the underchosen ones improve their chances of finding friends. He was convinced that if persons were placed in the same group who had chosen each other, then their spontaneity and creativity was bound to increase, no matter what the basis of choice.

The Sociogram

One of Moreno's sociometric diagrams of a "sociogram" is reproduced in Figure 7.1. Here he has pictured the pattern of interpersonal choice in one of the cottage families in the school for delinquent girls in New York. The circles in the diagram represent the girls in the cottage and the lines between them represent their choices of five other girls from the cottage with whom they most wanted to live. Although it was not done for this group, the subjects are also often asked whom they would reject. The rejections may then be pictured on the same or a different sociogram. The arrowhead on a line indicates the direction of choice. If two persons choose each other, the arrows are joined in a straight line with a dash across the center.

After the choices of each girl in cottage C3 had been pictured, the resulting choice pattern indicated the following characteristics of the 23 girls:

Type	Number	Identification
Isolated	5	BA, GM, RA, LY, TS
Unchosen	5	CM, JM, GL, RC, BN
Mutual attractions (pairs)	6	AE-HF, AE-PC, PC-PP, PC-YA, PC-KR, UT-SY
Chains	1	HF-AE-PC-KR-PP
Triangles	0	
Stars	1	LT (Note: LT is an "isolated star," as she chooses no one in return.)

Moreno describes this group as one with an extroverted group organization. Its special features are a large number of nonparticipating individuals, low group cohesion, and low differentiation between underchosen and overchosen members.

Choice Criteria

The criterion used in Moreno's study of the cottage (that is, choice of roommates) is similar to the criterion of "Whom would you choose as a friend?" that is used in many studies. Both criteria are rather general, but both would appear to lie primarily within the social-emotional area. A typical question involving a criterion in the task area is "Whom would you choose to work with?"

Subjects tend to make fewer choices in a friendship criterion than on a work criterion. However, correlations are high between choices based on each of these criteria, since there are some "great men" (Borgatta, Couch, and Bales, 1954) who actually have desirable traits in all other areas, and there are some subjects who will choose on a criterion important to them regardless of the experimenter's request. As a result there is often little difference no matter what criterion is proposed. Subjects who value task performance will choose others who are effective in the task and those who value social or emotional traits will choose on that basis. In general, social traits (such as warm, hostile, generous) are more important than nonsocial traits (such as happy, intelligent, hard-working) in determining attraction.

An example of choice based on the subject's own criterion rather than that of the experimenter is found in an experiment by E. G. French (1956) using 137 air corps personnel in their seventh week of training. The men were given a test designed to measure both achievement and affiliation motivation. They were then divided into groups of four to work on "important concept formation test." The groups were so constructed that three of the subjects had previously rated each other as "liked" and the fourth member as "not liked." All subjects first worked individually on a sorting task in which the disliked member was made to succeed and the other members to fail. The subjects were then asked to make one or two choices for a work partner to repeat the same task in pairs. On this sociometric rest the subjects who were high in achievement and low in affiliation motivation made significantly more single choices of the unliked members who appeared to be successful, while the subjects who were high in affiliation and low in achivment made significantly more choices of the two friends. Those who were high in both motivations made significantly more double choices involving both a friend and the successful person, while the subjects who were low in both motivations predominantly chose a friend.

In this study the use of sociometric test meets all the criteria suggested by Moreno, since a specific work criterion is used and the group is restructured on the basis of the choices; it is evident, however, that some subjects tend to disregard the criterion and choose on the basis of their predominant interpersonal need. An additional finding that the subjects in this experiment with high need for achievement differed from those with high need for affiliation in the extent to which they made "dislike" ratings in the first place suggests that the two types of individuals also have a different basis for choice on the more general criterion of "friend."

Different choice criteria also influence the form and content of interaction. In a study by Back (1951), the "cohesiveness" of two-man groups was manipulated by telling some pairs that they would or would not like each other, others that they would or would not receive a prize for the best group performance, and still others that they would or would not serve as a model of a highly productive group. Back found that when cohesiveness was based on personal attraction, group members tended to make the discussion into a long pleasant conversation; when it was based on task performance, the members tried to finish quickly and efficiently; and when it was based on group prestige, the members acted cautiously so that they would not endanger their status.

In another example, caseworkers in a welfare agency were asked to choose whom they would "respect as a colleague" and to whom they were "attracted as a sociable companion." Persons high on choices of respect were sought for consultation about casework matters, while those who were high on attraction were looked to for informal interaction (Blau, 1962).

Even though sociometric choices do vary to some extent with the criterion, the experimenter often pools the ratings made on several criteria so that the distinctions are lost. Most of the literature on interpersonal choice is summarized in this chapter without regard to specific criteria, although it is possible, in some cases, to illustrate the variations in the behavior of a subject which are associated with his choices based on different criteria.

Reciprocal Choice

When an investigator asks the subjects to rate all other members of the group using some criterion of choice, the data include not only those choices which the individuals have consciously made before the experimenter arrives on the scene but also those choices which have only been made for the purpose of the questionnaire, which played no major part in the development of the social structure. An individual who is ranked low by another individual may, therefore, but someone who is disliked, or someone who is relatively unknown to the first person. When group members are relative strangers, mutual choices may occur simply by chance. In general, however, choices are not at random, since in every group some persons are more chosen and some less than would be expected if only chance factors were operating.

Almost any indication of positive choice will be reciprocated, including simple agreement, using a person's name, touching, giving positive evaluations, helping, or rewarding in various ways. Reciprocation of choice will not appear, however, unless a sociometric question is asked which makes reciprocation of choice possible. For example, mutual choices would not be expected if subjects were asked to nominate the best potential leaders in the group. Mutual choice would be expected with a criterion of "sit next to" or "room with."

Basis of Friendship

Most people choose each other for a variety of reasons. The generalization that "birds of a feather flock together" is supported by most of the studies of friendship, although there is also evidence that "opposites attract." To sort out the conditions under which one or the other of these generalizations will hold, it is helpful to have some theory. Once more AGIL comes to our aid to provide a preliminary ordering to the voluminous literature on friendship. The first factor in friendship formation is *proximity*, since persons who never meet never become part of the same social system and therefore have no opportunity to form interpersonal relations. Once two persons are part of the same system, they may be attracted to each other because of biological traits (A), personality characteristics (G), common or reciprocal roles (I), or common values (L). We would expect the strongest interpersonal bonds to include all four system levels.

The evidence for the importance of *proximity* is as follows: persons who live near each other or are near each other on the job or in school become friends more often than persons who live or work farther apart. Once acquainted, persons who are attracted to each other seek each other out at lunch or other places of possible contact and so increase the chance of being together. Friendship groups continue longest if the members have a work relationship with each other.

Once two persons are part of the same social system, they may form a friendship on the basis of similar *biological traits* such as athletic ability or physical attractiveness, although physically attractive persons tend to be highly chosen by everyone.

It is even more likely that friends will have *personality characteristics* that are compatible in some way. Individuals with the same personality type tend to choose each other, and marriage partners with similar personality traits are found to be more satisfied with their spouses. Persons are also found to choose others whom they describe as having traits similar to their own positive traits and to reject others whom they describe as having traits similar to their own negative traits.

It is also possible that "congruence" of personality traits is more important than similarity. Two personality needs are "congruent" if they allow reciprocation; that is, dominant persons will choose those who are submissive, while those who prefer close interpersonal warmth will choose others who are similar in this trait rather than those who prefer distance (Secord and Backman, 1964).

Moving up to the social system level we find that friendships are formed on the basis of *common roles* such as those based on age, sex, and group position. Of course age and sex are also associated with biological traits, personality characteristics, and value systems, but with the advent of the various liberation movements in the 1970s it became apparent that social characteristics traditionally associated with age and sex (and also race) were not firmly fixed, but were roles that could be learned. However, as long as these role distinctions exist it will not be surprising to find that interpersonal attraction will be influenced by traditional norms.

Finally, at the cultural level, a friendship is more likely to continue if the individuals have *common interests* or *values*. For example, in a study of the Supreme Court of the United States as a small group, three cliques were identified. The membership in these cliques appeared to be related to the ideology of the judges (Snyder, 1958). Religion, ethnic group, and social class may provide a common value system.

One way to look at the formation of friendship bonds between persons is to consider the exchanges that are made or that can be called upon within the friendship pair. Friends try to keep their relationship balanced by exchanging (I) affection or (L) respect for other valued forms of behavior such as (A) information or (G) power (Blau, 1960, 1962; Davis, 1963; Newcomb, 1963; Feather, 1967). Thus submissive persons choose those who will provide direction (Secord and Backman, 1964), or a person will increase liking for another person in anticipation of cooperation in a mutual task (Darley and Berscheid, 1967).

Morale and Cohesiveness

As well as being an indication of the informal structure of a group, interpersonal choices can also be used to form an index of morale or cohesiveness. Groups are said to have high morale or to be cohesive if members are highly attracted to the group. The terms *morale* and *cohesiveness* have generally been used interchangeably.

The term *cohesiveness* is favored by those whose work follows the pattern set by Lewin. They use an index of attractiveness to the group that is based on one choice or some combination of choices in the task and social-emotional areas. One should be cautious, however, about combining the results of studies that use different sociometric criteria for their indices. Attraction based on "likability," for example, may lead to different forms of interaction than attraction based on "task ability." If the group members come together with work as the primary goal, they will probably spend little time on social activity in contrast to a group formed on an affectional basis (see Back, 1951, noted above).

An index of the attractiveness of the group for its members is often desired since the extent of attractiveness is also found to be related to the significance of the group as a reference group for judgments about the self and others, as indicated in Chapter 6. Once an individual has dropped out of a group that has lost its attraction, the group will no longer be a positive reference group.

In industrial plants where the personal bonds are well established and newly recruited members are easily accepted, there is less labor turnover than in plants that are similar in geographic location, technology, and labor force, but where bonds between members are weak and no informal group standards are enforced. High in-group choice is also related to effective performance on field problems in infantry rifle squads. However, a cohesive group may be less productive if the members have agreed to lower the production rate in opposition to the norms of the larger organization.

In an extensive study of group cohesiveness in industrial work groups, data were drawn from 228 groups ranging in size from five to fifty members in a machine factory. The results indicated that members of high-cohesive work groups exhibited less anxiety than members of low-cohesive work groups. In the high-cohesive groups there was also less variation in productivity among the members, although the high-cohesive groups differed more frequently and in greater amounts from the plant norm of productivity than did the low-cohesive groups. The amount of cohesiveness in a group was positively related to the degree of prestige that the members of the group attributed to their own jobs, the opportunities for interaction as measured by the size of the group (that is, the larger the group the fewer the opportunities for interaction), and the length of time the members had been together on the job (Seashore, 1954).

Psychegroups

In the discussion of criteria for sociometric choice it was noted that persons generally make more choices on a "work" or "task" criterion than they do in a "friendship" or "social-emotional" criterion. In an early sociometric paper, Jennings (1947) referred to these two types of relationships as the "sociogroup" and the "psychegroup." Although a group composed of mutual "task" choices might be best for ordinary everyday goal attainment, Stein (1974: 264-165) in his summary of the roles played by different types of intermediaries in support of individual creativity stresses the part played by the persons who constitute the "social-emotional" choices, or the "psychegroup."

The importance of various types of intermediaries in the creative process will be considered in more detail in Chapter 10; however, in brief they often include: (1) a *patron* who supports the creative individual and makes it possible for that person to devote time to creativity, (2) the *psychegroup* which plays a key part at the time the individual is creating, (3) *entrepreneurs* who provide the risk capital, (4) *executives* who organize the social and physical environment to supply the resources for creativity, (5) *experts* who judge the significance of the contribution, (6) *transmission agents* such as county agricultural agents or Peace Corps volunteers who spread the new ideas, and (7) *opinion leaders* who influence the receptivity of the community (Stein, 1974: 261-290).

If the creative person can bypass the *patron* and find other means of support, then the *psychegroup* becomes the most significant part of the whole process, since without the support of these individuals at the crucial time there would be no creation for the other intermediaries to bring to the community. To provide some indication of the importance of the psychegroup, Stein's summary of his impressions after reviewing the literature on creativity is quoted in the next few paragraphs.*

"The psychegroup is a reference group for the creative individual. It is generally an informal group of supporters that gathers around or is sought out by the creative individual. They and the creative person are bound together by professional ties or long-term friendships. The creative person can go to the psychegroup throughout the various stages of the creative process for emotional support, advice, criticism, clarification, or even to discuss the testing of some of his (or her) ideas. Discussions within this group may be one of the early manifestations that new ideas are developing or that still newer and different ones are yet to come. The size of the group may vary from one to several persons. A particularly good example of a psychegroup is the group of artists who gathered around Diaghilev in the early nineteenth century. Dancers, painters, musicians, and writers, many of whom later became foremost in their fields, helped and stimulated each other in the face of a skeptical public.

"Freud's relationship with Fliess, when it was still a positive one, is an example of a psyche dyad. One of the values of this relationship for Freud is reflected in the following excerpt from one of his letters to Fliess. The letter was written to tell Fliess that he (Freud) was unable to keep a meeting in Berlin:

> I do so most unwillingly, because I expected a great deal from meeting you. Though otherwise quite satisfied, happy if you like, I feel very isolated, scientifically blunted, stagnant, and resigned. When I talked to you, and saw that you thought something of me, I actually started thinking something of myself, and the picture of confident energy which you offered was not without its effect. I should also have profited professionally from meeting you, and perhaps I should also have benefited from the Berlin atmosphere, because for years now I have been without anyone who could teach me anything and have settled down more or less exclusively to the treatment of neuroses.

"Relationships with older individuals, masters of the field in which an individual works, although qualitatively different from those established with his (or her) peers, may also constitute psychegroups. Such relationships may be on the decline in the contemporary scene.

"Dahlberg, speaking as a writer says, 'The most prodigious mishap of the young American writer is that he has no Master, or an elder of letters

*From M. I. Stein, *Stimulating Creativity, Vol. I.* New York: Academic Press. Copyright © 1974. Used by permission of both author and publisher.

to guide him; and so he relies wholly upon himself, a very unreliable teacher. I was lucky; I knew Theodore Dreiser and Sherwood Anderson.'

"To have a psychegroup with which to communicate openly and frankly can be extremely valuable to the creative person. He (or she) does not feel evaluated by this group and hence can freely alter ideas already expressed or receive encouragement to go off to new uncharted areas of creative endeavor."

Anyone who wishes more documentation of the part played by the psychegroup can search through the biographies of persons who have been judged to be creative. In the small sample that I examined I found that biographers are understandably more interested in the development of the ideas, style of painting, or whatever of the creative person than they are in the part played by friends. Nevertheless, one may occasionally catch glimpses of the type of support that has been given at all phases of the creative process. In the case of Einstein, for example, Bernstein (1973) included in his biography a line or two at various points giving some idea of the part played by friends and close associates, even though Einstein by his own account and those of others was solitary and introspective as a child and relatively isolated from personal contacts as an adult.*

In a letter to Queen Elizabeth in 1939 Einstein wrote: "I have hit upon a hopeful trail, which I follow painfully but steadfastly in company with a few youthful fellow workers" [Bernstein, 1973: 11]

In another reminiscence Einstein recalled the part played by a friend at school who took careful lecture notes so that Einstein would not have to attend the lectures and could spend most of the time in the physics laboratory where he was fascinated by the direct contact with experience:

There were altogether only two examinations [at school]; aside from these, one could just do as one pleased. This was especially true if one had a friend, as I did, who attended the lectures regularly and who worked over their content conscientiously. This gave one freedom in the choice of persuits until a few months before the examination, a freedom which I enjoyed to a great extent and have gladly taken into the bargain the bad conscience connected with it as by far the lesser evil. . . . It is, in fact, nothing short of a miracle that the modern methods of instruction have not yet entirely strangled the holy curiosity of inquiry [Bernstein, 1973: 78].

Or again, Einstein once remarked that until he had published his paper on relativity in 1905, he had never been in correspondence with, or met, a real physicist. The only person he was able to discuss ideas with until he was thirty years old was Michaelangelo Besso, and engineer, whom Einstein had known since his student days. He was also an employee of the patent office where Einstein worked before Einstein's scientific contributions were recognized and he was given a university post. In the last sentence of his 1905 paper, Einstein wrote:

> In conclusion I wish to say that in working at the problem here dealt with I have had the loyal assistance of my friend and colleague M. Besso, and that I am indebted to him for several valuable suggestions [Bernstein, 1973: 82].

A more detailed glimpse of the actual process of interaction between friends in the interest of creativity is given by Bernstein in a letter written in 1916 by Ehrenfest in Leyden who was present when Einstein visited Lorentz. This was just after Einstein had put his theory of relativity in its final form and he wanted very much to talk to Lorentz, who although in retirement in his early sixties was still working intensly on research. Ehrenfest wrote the following account of the meeting (Bernstein, 1973: 208-209):

> In his usual way Lorentz saw to it first at dinner that Einstein felt himself enveloped in a warm and cheerful atmosphere of human sympathy. Later, without any hurry, we went up to Lorentz's cozy and simple study. The best easy chair was carefully pushed in place next to the large work table for the esteemed guest. Calmly, and to forestall any impatience, a cigar was provided for the guest, and only then did Lorentz begin quietly to formulate a finely polished question concerning Einstein's theory of the bending of light in a gravitational field. Einstein listened to the exposition, sitting comfortably in the easy chair and smoking, nodding happily, taking pleasure in the masterly way Lorentz had discovered, by studying his works, all the enormous difficulties that Einstein had to overcome before he could lead his readers to their destination, as he did in his papers, by a more direct and less troublesome route. But as Lorentz spoke on and on, Einstein began to puff less frequently on his cigar, and he sat up straighter and more intently in his armchair. And when Lorentz finished, Einstein sat bent over the slip of paper on which Lorentz had written mathematical formulas to accompany his words as he spoke. The cigar was out, and Einstein pensively twisted his fingers in a lock of hair over his right ear. Lorentz, however, sat smiling at an Einstein completely lost in meditation, exactly the way a father looks at a particularly beloved son—full of secure confidence

that the youngster will crack the nut he has given him, but eager to see how. It took quite a while but suddenly Einstein's head shot up joyfully; he "had it!" Still a bit of give and take, interrupting one another; a partial disagreement, very quick clarification and a complete mutual understanding, and then both men with beaming eyes skimming over the shining riches of the new theory.

Near the end of his own life Einstein wrote of Lorentz, "For me personally he meant more than all of the others I have met along life's journey" (Bernstein, 1973: 209).

Summary

When Moreno introduced the term "sociometry" to refer to the analysis of patterns of interpersonal choice in groups, he hoped the information would be used to reorganize groups for maximum spontaneity and creativity. This would be done by placing persons who had chosen each other in the same group. The criterion for choice makes a difference since persons who have chosen each other on a "task" criterion will generally be more effective in work, while those who have chosen each other on a "social-emotional" criterion will pay more attention to interpersonal relations. Although relatively few social scientists have actually reorganized groups on the basis of their research, an extensive literature has been produced on the patterns of interpersonal choice and on the reasons why persons choose each other.

Almost any indication of positive choice will be reciprocated. Persons who become good friends tend to be similar or complementary at four system levels, provided they have some chance to meet in the first place. Persons may be attracted to each other because of biological traits (A), personality characteristics (G), common or reciprocal roles (I), or common values (L), with the strongest bonds involving all levels.

Groups that have a high level of interpersonal attraction have high *morale* and are termed *cohesive.* High cohesiveness is generally associated with high productivity, unless the group members have conspired to lower production.

As an adjunct to the creative process for individuals, Stein has noted the importance of various types of intermediaries who play a part at different stages of the process. A crucial role is played by an individual's *psychegroup*, the informal group of supporters that gathers around or is sought out by the creative individual. Several quotations from Einstein document the important part that close friends played at several stages in his career.

Chapter 8
Roles

In its more formal definition the term *role* refers to the set of expectations that group members share concerning the behavior of a person who occupies a given position in a group where the positions usually represent specialties related to the task of the group. However, in practice, the term *role* is used to represent any set of behaviors that a person typically performs in a group. Thus any aspect of an individual's behavior that is an expression of personality can come to be expected by other group members and become part of the individual's role. Although early research of groups, especially on children, often described "individual" or "self-oriented" roles as if the only role of some individuals was to satisfy their own needs (Benne and Sheats, 1948), other formulations by Redl (1942), Bion (1961), and Stock and Thelen (1958) suggest that all roles in the group serve some function. However, some of these roles, especially the ones that allow members to deal with emotional themes, may not be recognized as part of the "official" group culture.

Task and Social-Emotional Roles in Terms of AGIL

The most common division of roles that has been described in small discussion or work groups, as well as families viewed as small groups, is specialization in the task and social-emotional areas (Slater, 1955; Bales, 1958). In terms of AGIL, the "task" specialist (either leader or follower) concentrates in the *adaptive* (A) and *goal-attainment* (G) areas, while the "social-emotional" specialist concentrates in the *pattern maintenance* (L) and *integrative* (I) areas. Bales has observed this distinction most clearly in small laboratory groups in which members have a high degree of agreement at the end of the meeting on the relative amount of interaction in each of these areas exhibited by group members. These groups appear to recognize

	Universalism Neutrality	Particularism Affectivity
Specificity Performance	A — Adaptation Universalism Specificity	G — Goal attainment Affectivity Performance
Diffuseness Quality	L — Pattern maintenance Quality Neutrality	I — Integration Diffuseness Particularism

Figure 8.1 Relationship between Pattern Variables and Four Functional Areas

two kinds of leaders: one an "idea" person who concentrates on the task and plays a more aggressive role and the other a "best-liked" person who concentrates on social-emotional problems of group process and members' satisfaction, giving emotional rewards, and playing a more passive role.

These roles of task and social-emotional specialties may actually be joined in one person. On the one hand, Borgatta, Couch, and Bales (1954) have observed that in some laboratory groups there are "great men" who are able to play all the necessary parts. On the other hand Blake and Mouton (1969: 61), who specialize in management development, consider that the ideal manager has a concern both for production and for people.

A slightly more complicated model for the analysis of roles is to consider the possibility that some leaders and followers will specialize in each of the four functional areas. That is, some will deal primarily with the provision of facilities (A), some with problem solutions relative to the group's goals (G), some with the provision of solidarity or norms (I), and some with the provision of basic categories or ultimate values (L).

Since there are different, and in some cases contradictory, sets of expectations for behavior in each of these four roles, some role conflict may occur if the same person tries to play more than one role. The general nature of the orientation required by each role can be seen in Figure 8.1 that shows the relationship between each of the roles and Parson's "pattern variables." The four sets of pattern variables are (Miner, 1968: 178):

- Affectivity (involving immediate self-gratification) vs. neutrality (requiring deferment of gratification)
- Specificity (narrow scope of relationship vs. diffuseness (broad scope of relationship)

- Universalism (action governed by general standards) vs. particularism (reference scheme peculiar to actors in the relationship)
- Quality (based on what a person is) vs. performance (based on what a person can do)

In Figure 8.1 the two columns of the fourfold paradigm involve a distinction between universalism and neutrality on the one hand and particularism and affectivity on the other. For the two rows the distinction is between specificity and performance and quality and diffuseness. Cross-cutting these sets of variables gives four characteristics for each cell. However Parsons (1949: 413) has suggested that two of them are more salient in each case. Thus we can consider that the predominant characteristics for the specializations for each of the roles are:

A—Adaptation: Universalism and specificity
G—Goal attainment: Affectivity and performance
I—Integration: Diffuseness and particularism
L—Pattern maintenance: Quality and neutrality

As an illustration of these four major types of roles, a case study is included at the end of this chapter in which Santiago Genovés as founder of the expedition (L) of the raft *Acali* to cross the Atlantic Ocean, also trys to play the roles of father (I) for the family, captain (G) of the vessel, and scientist (A) observing the behavior of crew members, with minimal success.

If one wishes to consider the possibility of subroles within each of the major areas, then the situation is more complex, and several alternative schemes are possible (Parsons, 1949: 413; Loubser, 1976: 247). One example is the paradigm of eight types of leaders that has been proposed by Olmsted (Olmsted and Hare, 1978: 139-144). The relationship between each of these eight types and the AGIL categories is indicated in Figure 8.2. In each cell of the figure a distinction is made between the processes of *differentiation* and *integration*. The role associated with *differentiation* is indicated by the letter "a" and the role associated with *integration* by the letter "b." This distinction, Olmsted notes, is inherent in any system made up of parts. A *system* consists of parts that are in some way different from one another in nature or function. These parts must be coordinated if the system is to maintain itself as a system rather than as a collection of units. Differentiation is a centrifugal process and integration a centripetal process. Moreover, differentiation is associated with specialization of parts (or specialized roles in the case of the small group) while integration is associated with generalization (or generalized roles).

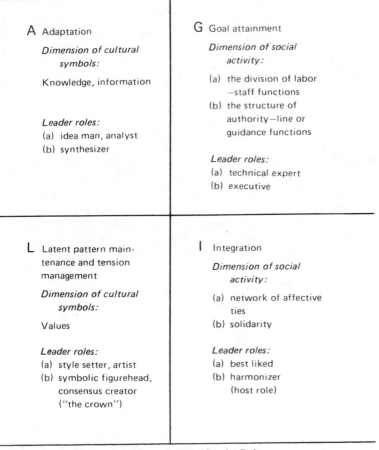

Figure 8.2 Paradigm of Group Dimensions and Leader Roles
SOURCE: M. S. Olmsted and A. P. Hare, *The Small Group* (New York: Random House, Inc., 1978), p. 141. Reprinted by permission of the publisher.

The most familiar case of differentiation and integration is in the goal attainment (G) sector of Figure 8.2 where, in many formal organizations, there is a specialization in "staff" and "line" functions. In the military, for example, the "staff" officers serve as technical experts while the "line" officers actually direct the troops in battle. Within each cell in Figure 8.2 this distinction is indicated under the subheading of "leader roles." The "staff" function is labeled as "a" and the "line" function as "b." The examples given for the goal attainment area in Figure 8.2 are (a) technical expert and (b) executive.

Continuing around the other three cells of Figure 8.2, in the adaptive (A) sector one can see a distinction between the role of analyst (A), who has a flow of original ideas, and a synthesizer (b), who is adept at putting together the contributions of others. In the integrative (I) sector we have the role of "best-liked" person (a), who is the focus of "personal" affective bonds, and the person who unites the group into a solidary whole, the harmonizer or host (b). The differentiating effect of having "best-liked" persons in groups is most clearly seen when there are more than one of them, thus often dividing the group into two or more subgroups around these "sociometric stars." Finally in the pattern maintenance sector (L) the specialized differentiating role (a) is here represented by the "style setter" who defines the attributes of prestigious living and the artist who refines old values into new ones (that is, provides for creativity). The more generalized integrating role (b) is that of the figurehead, who rather than doing something, stands for something. This symbolic role, which represents the moral consensus of the group, can be held either by an individual or by an abstract principle such as the crown, the flag, or the tribal totem. These individuals, or principles, serve to legitimize the value system and social organization of the group.

In effect, Olmsted has provided examples of two of the four subtypes within each of the four functional areas. Since the "staff" function provides resources or energy for the sector it can be coded adaptive, "a." Since the "line" function provides the guidance it can be coded as goal attainment, "g." Thus the technical expert represents the adaptive specialty within the goal attainment sector, or "G_a" and the executive represents the goal attainment specialty within the goal attainment sector, or "G_g," and so on around the other three sectors.

The various typologies given so far are described in terms of their functional content (AGIL). The basic assumption is that if a group is to survive as a group, to solve everyday problems and to be creative sometimes, these roles must be filled by one or more persons in the group, since they contribute to the various stages of group development and steps in the problem-solving and creative process. They focus on *what* is expected of the persons who fill the roles. But there is another way of looking at roles: by focusing on the process, that is on *how* the role is played. This second approach is represented by the work of Bales and others who have had a longstanding interest in the *process* of interaction. Of course, as noted in Chapter 2, there turns out to be a connection between the two approaches, since a focus on each type of *content* is typically associated with a style of *process*. In the next few pages we look at roles again, this time from the perspective of three and four dimensions of interaction.

TABLE 8.1   Composite Profiles in Percentages of 44 Top Men on Idea Ranking and 44 Top Men on Like Ranking for the Same Sessions

		Initiated		Received	
	Interaction category	Idea Men	Best-liked men	Idea men	Best-liked men
Area A:	Shows solidarity	3.68	4.41	2.57	3.15
Positive	Shows tension release	5.15	6.98	7.95	9.20
reactions	Shows agreement	14.42	16.83	23.29	18.27
Area B:	Gives suggestion	8.97	6.81	7.01	7.22
Problem-solving	Gives opinion	32.74	28.69	25.52	31.09
attempts	Gives orientation	18.54	17.91	14.06	14.54
Area C:	Asks orientation	3.04	3.71	3.62	2.80
Questions	Asks opinion	1.84	2.94	1.94	1.74
	Asks suggestion	.93	1.33	.85	.84
Area D:	Shows disagreement	8.04	7.60	10.65	9.35
Negative	Shows tension increase	1.92	2.16	1.59	1.35
reactions	Shows antagonism	.73	.63	.95	.45

SOURCE: Philip E. Slater, "Role Differentiation in Small Groups," *American Sociological Review* 20 (1955): 305. Copyright © 1955 by the American Sociological Association. Reprinted by permission of the publisher.

Roles as Combinations of Three Dimensions of Interaction

In an early and popular article on roles, Benne and Sheats (1948) described a set of "functional roles of group members" many of which were single categories of acts. Thus they observed that one person might be an "opinion giver" or another a "blocker." However, a more common approach was to give a cluster of behaviors or a "profile" of behavior as an indication of a type of role. As an example of the profile approach we can consider the profiles of "idea men" and "best-liked men" observed by Bales and Slater (Slater, 1955: 305; Bales, 1958: 442) as given in Table 8.1.

Table 8.1 shows the composite profiles of 44 matched session-pairs of persons who had received the highest ranking in their groups on giving ideas, but who were not the best liked, and persons who were the best liked, but were not at the top of the idea ranking. In general, the idea person tends to initiate more interaction in Area B, problem-solving attempts, and the best-liked person in Area A, positive reactions. The idea person also disagrees somewhat more and shows a little more antagonism, while the best-liked person asks more questions and shows more tension.

In the profiles of acts received, the situation is largely reversed, with the idea person receiving more agreement, questions, and negative reactions, while the best-liked person receives more problem-solving attempts, more solidarity, and more tension release. The general picture is thus one of specialization and complementarity, with the idea person concentrating on the task and playing a more aggressive role, while the best-liked person concentrates more on social-emotional problems, giving rewards and playing a more passive role (Bales, 1958: 441-442).

The difficulty with this type of profile is that the usual category systems have more than six categories and as a result some categories appear with very low frequencies so that differences between profiles are hard to establish on an act-by-act basis. Further, it is difficult to display the profiles for all group members at the same time in a way that makes meaningful comparisons obvious. These difficulties are overcome when one shifts to a dimensional approach involving only a few dimensions.

The most elaborate scheme for analysis of behavior, roles, images, the situation, and indeed almost all important aspects of the social system, has been developed by Bales and his colleagues. The basic three-dimensional scheme is set out in the 1970 volume *Personality and Interpersonal Behavior* and an even more comprehensive approach presented in the 1979 volume *SYMLOG: A System for the Multiple Level Observation of Groups*. In these books Bales provides checklists and category systems that make it possible to rate or rank each member of a group on the three dimensions of interaction: upward-downward, positive-negative, and forward-backward (see Chapter 2 for more details on the meaning of these dimensions). Bales is then able to plot the position of each member of a group on a Field Diagram such as the one in Figure 8.3 that shows Bales and the other members of one' of his "self-analytic" groups of undergraduates at Harvard University (Bales et al. 1979: 53).

In Figure 8.3 the horizontal axis represents the negative-positive dimension (from left to right) and the vertical axis the forward-backward dimension (from top to bottom). The third dimension of upward-downward is indicated by the size of the circle that surrounds the dot (small circle) locating a person on the other two dimensions. The larger circles represent the more upward (dominant) members. The actual rating on the upward-downward dimension is also shown below the name of each group member. For example, Bales (RFB), in the upper-right quadrant, is noted as "6U" or "6 upward." Just below him on the diagram is Lain who is "3D" or "3 downward."

Also shown in Figure 8.3 are some lines and circles that represent the extent and direction of *polarization* and *unification* in the group. The *Line*

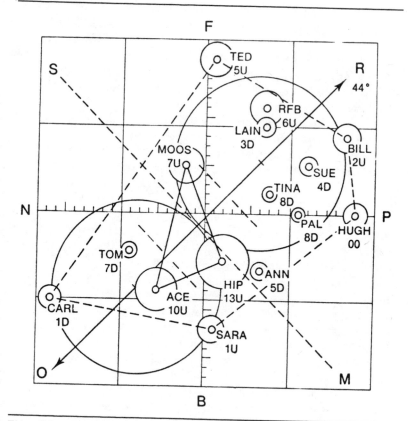

Figure 8.3 RFB's Field Diagram, with Dominant Triangle and Perimeter (Expansion Multiplier = 1.199)

SOURCE: Reprinted with permission of Macmillan Publishing Co., Inc. from *SYMLOG: A Manual for the Case Study of Groups* by Robert F. Bales, Stephen P. Cohen, and Stephen A. Williamson. Copyright © 1976 by The Free Press, a Division of Macmillan Publishing Co., Inc.

of Polarization (solid line tipped with arrowheads at either end) passes across the Field Diagram in a direction that is located by a procedure described in Bales's book. One end of the Line of Polarization is marked with an "R," which stands for *Reference Direction.* The other end of the Line of Polarization is marked with an "O," which stands for *Opposite Direction.* In this case, since Bales made the ratings, the reference direction is taken to be in the direction of the subgroup with which he is associated. If one was considering the ratings of Ace, in the lower left quadrant, the reference direction would be the other way around. To find the reference direction for the group as a whole one might use the average member rating, or the ratings of the most dominant members. However, the group may in fact be a composite of several subgroups, each with its own direction.

A dashed line, called the *Line of Balance*, passes across the Field Diagram at right angles to the Line of Polarization. One end of the Line of Balance is marked with an "M," which stands for *Mediator Direction* and the other end with an "S," which stands for *Scapegoat Direction.* These terms have reference to the possible social-psychological significance to the rater of any image found far out in one direction or the other.

There are two large circles on the diagram, one on each side of the Line of Balance, each centered on the Line of Polarization. These represent the two polar fields of polarization. The circle nearest the "R" is called the *Reference Circle* and the one nearest the "O," the *Opposite Circle.*

There are also two short dashed lines on either side of the Line of Balance and parallel to it. Between them is the *Swing Area.* In the case of conflict persons in this area may be rejected by both sides or they may decide to "swing" their votes to one side or the other.

Two other kinds of relationships are also indicated on the diagram. The center points of the circles representing the three most dominant persons are connected with solid lines to show the *Dominant Triangle,* since these persons have most to do with the direction of group activity. In this case Moos, Hip, and Ace form the dominant triangle.

A dotted line connects those persons who are most distant from the center of the total constellation of image points. This is called the *Perimeter.* The Perimeter may call attention to some moderate or low participators who are nevertheless salient because they are "far-out" in their given direction (Bales et al., 1979: 38-57).

Bales offers six heuristic hypotheses as a way to begin to predict some of the developments in a group once a diagram has been drawn based on observations in early sessions of the group, or perhaps on personality assessments or self-ratings made before the first meeting of the group. The heuristic hypotheses are as follows (Bales et al., 1979: 58-108):

(1) Dominant members may clash early, especially if they are in different quadrants of the space.
(2) Far-out members may clash sooner or later, that is, in the middle period of a chronically polarized group.
(3) Downward members may come in last, although the leader could help bring them in.
(4) Salient images may polarize or unify the group.
(5) Polarization may tend to create leaders and subgroups.
(6) Polarization may be neutralized by mediation, scapegoating, or domination.

In his 1970 book, Bales devotes several pages to the description of each of the 26 types of behavior representing combinations of the three dimensions, including the person's self-perception and how the person is seen by others, the person's place in the interaction network, ideas and values, quality of interaction, conflicts and coalitions, personality traits, perception of parents, and effect on group satisfaction. The 1979 volume adds descriptions of the images and value judgments associated with each type. As a brief indication of the 26 descriptions, the summary paragraphs for two types, UB and DF, are given below.*

Type UB (upward-backward): Toward Value Relativism and Expression. The member located in the upward-backward part of the group space by his fellow members seems ascendant and expressive, nontask oriented, perhaps unconventional or even deviant. He seems neither clearly friendly nor unfriendly, but entertaining, joking, dramatic, relativistic, free in his associations, taking pleasure in play, activity, novelty, and creativity. In the realization of his own values he seems to be trying to move toward value-relativism and expression of underlying emotions and feelings. "Life is more a festival than a workshop for moral discipline."

DF (downward-forward): Toward Self-Knowledge and Subjectivity. The member located in the downward-forward part of the group space by his fellow members seems submissive, dutiful, and conventional, wishing to follow a value- and task-oriented leader. He seems neither friendly nor unfriendly, but strictly impersonal, affectively neutral, inhibited, cautious, introverted, persistently hardworking, and fearful of disapproval and guilt. He is concerned with his inner feelings, his thoughts, impulses, and controls. In the realization of his own values he seems to be trying to move toward more complete knowledge of himself and more subjective completeness. "No time is better spent that devoted to thinking about the ultimate purposes of life."*

Given any of the above schemes for the analysis of roles, or the four dimensional scheme that follows, it is possible to look at other role typologies suggested in the literature to see where they fit in the interpersonal space. For example, Cloyd (1964) identified six patterns of behavior in discussion groups without reference to any particular dimensions and without assigning them names. Some of the traits listed in each cluster by Cloyd are given here, together with the letters and words representing Bales's type that seems to be essentially the same:

Cloyd's Cluster	*Bales's Role*
1. Aggressive, self-confident, gets things started.	UF — Upward-forward
2. Modest, shy, ill at ease.	DB — Downward-backward
3. Friendly, objective.	P — Positive
4. Idealistic, argumentative.	N — Negative
5. Makes humorous remarks, challenges others' opinions.	UP — Upward-backward
6. Dependable, constructive.	DF — Downward-forward

The short descriptions of the UB (upward-backward) and DF (downward-forward) types that were given above provide a sample comparison. We note that in terms of Bales's three dimensional space, each pair of roles identified by Cloyd represent two types that are opposite each other and are independent of each other (orthogonal), however they do not begin to cover the whole space. In the leadership area, for example, Cloyd does not identify a person who is UPF (upward-positive-forward) or a "natural leader" nor does he identify a person who is UNF (upward-negative-forward), a "dictator," or the other five upward types that Bales has described. This is probably a reflection of group composition, the type of task the group had, and the length of time the members had been together. Thus we would not expect the members of all groups to cover all positions in the interpersonal space.

In order to visualize the types of roles to expect in a group we can use a basketball team as an analogy. The space the five members have to cover is defined by the length and width of the court and the highest point that the tallest and/or highest jumping person can reach. As a collectivity the members on one team have to be able to handle the ball in any part of the space and they also have to be able to defend against activity of the other team in any part of the space. No one member need be able to do all of these things, but their combined roles must be equal to the task.

For groups (or individuals) to be creative in their problem-solving, Stein records that they must be able to deal with four stages in the creative process (Stein, 1974: 259-267):

(1) Preparatory stage: Information must be gathered about the general problem area. For each individual member this can include the education of a lifetime.

(2) Hypothesis formation: The group must be clear about the general nature of the problem that requires a solution and must be able to formulate specific hypotheses concerning a solution.

(3) Hypothesis testing: From available possibilities, one solution must eventually be selected as the most "elegant."

(4) Communication of results: The new object, form of organization, or idea must be put to use by the persons for whom it was intended. The effectiveness of the group in marketing the product of their creative efforts will depend on the resistance to change in the area in which they have been working.

The stages identified by Stein are essentially the same as those involved in ordinary problem-solving. Hoffman (1979), for example, outlines five phases in problem-solving. The main difference between the two processes lies in the amount of creativity in the solution. Hoffman's phases are:

(1) *Defining* the problem or setting goals.
(2) *Specifying* the barriers to be overcome.
(3) *Generating* alternative solutions.
(4) *Evaluating* the solutions.
(5) *Adopting a solution.*

By combining their roles, group members must be able to handle all of the tasks implied by each of the problem-solving stages in the creative process in their turn. Initially the dependable workers are required to build a body of facts, then the nonconformists have their day since it is necessary to have a "breakthrough" from the older patterns of thought, then the systematizers come forward to clarify relationships and to make sure that all relevant variables have been included, next the critics help narrow down the possibilities and the supporters provide encouragement to keep the group on the task, and finally the salespersons come forward to market the product. Whenever anyone takes up a prominent role as a "protagonist" or theme carrier for that stage, there is an opportunity for someone else to take a contrasting role as an "antagonist." Thus we may see pairs of roles emerging, as in Cloyd's analysis.

Farris (1972) provides an example of the way in which group members take complementary roles in the creative process. He interviewed 117 scientists who were members of small research and development teams. The scientists reported that their colleagues provided technical information and helped them think out technical problems while their supervisors provided critical evaluation.

Although Bales's three-dimensional scheme (or the four-dimensional scheme) does a great deal to bring the complexity of interpersonal behavior into some manageable arena, the typologies based on ratings of a few dimensions may not be sensitive enough to pick up fine distinctions in roles where these are important for a particular task. In such a case, a category system like Bales's original 12 categories might be an additional aid. For example, if one takes the profiles given in Table 8.1 for the "idea" person and the "best-liked" person and projects them in three dimensions using the transformations suggested by Bales (1968: 468, 1970: 91-135) then the major differences noted in the profiles disappear. Both types turn out to be primarily *forward,* with the "idea" person more so than the "best-liked" person, and both slightly *upward* to the same extent. In contrast to what one would expect from the role titles, the "best-liked" person is neutral on the positive-negative dimension while the "idea" person is slightly positive. Of course Bales and Slater observed the two role types using the 12 categories some years before Bales started using the three dimensions and the transformations he proposed are only to be considered approximations, still this does illustrate that fact that you may lose some detail as you shift from the more detailed categories to a broader dimensional analysis.

Roles in Four Dimensions

Since Bales has done so much to show how interpersonal behavior can be understood in terms of three dimensions, why go on to four? I have already given one motivation in Chapter 2 where I noted that it was difficult to combine the four AGIL categories together with the three dimensions of Bales. Four dimensions gave the possibility of a better fit. However, it was still possible that the three dimensions might be used with profit when the AGIL analysis was not simultaneously involved. I tried again to use the three dimensional scheme in 1977 in connection with a study of "Images of victims and victimizers in the onset of genocide" (Hare, 1978b). I was doing research in Israel at the time, and found that as I tried to use Bales's typology to study terrorists, nonviolent protesters, military deserters, and other "deviant" types that appear in Israel and elsewhere, that Bales placed some types together in the same box in his 26-box design that seemed better kept apart. Granted that any category scheme may create some strange bedfellows, still I wondered once more if a four-dimensional scheme might not bring out more useful distinctions.

The specific problem that I encountered with Bales's system was that he grouped pacifists and nonviolent protesters in the same category as defectors and military deserters, namely downward and backward. From my experience with individuals and groups engaged in nonviolent action (Hare and Blumberg, 1968, 1977, 1980) I considered nonviolent protesters and deserters to be sufficiently different to warrant appearing in different boxes. The difference seemed to lie along the serious-expressive dimension.

If I had followed Bales's example and included three categories for each of the four dimensions, I would have generated 81 role types. Even dropping the middle (average) type, this would seem to be more different-iation than most observers needed. However, if one cuts each dimension in

**TABLE 8.2   16 Types of Roles (Images) Classified According to
Four Dimensions of Interpersonal Behavior**

*Dimensional code**	*Examples of roles (images)*
1. UPSC	Natural leader
2. UNSC	Dictator, prison warden
3. UNEC	Exhibitionist
4. UPEC	Inspirational leader, old-fashioned mother, doctor
5. DPSC	Nurse, mail man, over achiever
6. DNSC	Spy, informer
7. DNEC	Critic, help-rejecting-complainer
8. DPEC	Clinging vine, yes-man
9. UPSA	Idealist, agent of change
10. UNSA	Anarchist, revolutionary
11. UNEA	Playboy, motorcycle bum
12. UPEA	Joker, court jester
13. DPSA	Pacifist, nonviolent resister
14. DNSA	Skeptic
15. DNEA	Defector, deserter, rebel
16. DPEA	Kept woman, gigolo

*Code: U Upward (Dominant)   –   D Downward (Submissive)
                P Positive   –   N Negative
                S Serious   –   E Expressive
                C Conforming   –   A Anti (non) conforming

the middle to create two categories, representing the two ends of each continuum, then the resulting typology of 16 role (image) types is manageable and less complicated than Bales's 26 types.

The four dimensional code together with some examples of the roles (or images) associated with each type are given in Table 8.2. Note that when a role type is *both serious* and *conforming* or *both expressive* and *anticonforming* the type is the same as that described by Bales in his analysis using three dimensions (1970; Bales, Cohen, and Williamson, 1979). In these cases Bales's descriptions of each type can be used. Even in those types where the role combines *serious* with *anticonforming* or *expressive* with *conforming,* one can sometimes see that Bales was in fact basing a distinction on either the serious-expressive dimension or on the conforming-anticonforming dimension, although in his theoretical description of *forward-backward* he treated the two dimensions as one. When this is the case, one can again use Bales's work as a source of hypotheses about the role type in four dimensions.

In the four-dimensional typology the pacifists and nonviolent protesters appear as downward (submissive), positive, serious, and anti(non)conforming (DPSA) while the military deserters are downward, negative, expressive, and anticonforming (DNEA). Whereas Bales placed the two types together as being neither very positive or very negative, the four-dimensional system forces the choice so that the nonviolent protesters are coded as generally positive and the deserters as generally negative. Although both are anticonforming, the nonviolent protesters seem serious and group-oriented in their advocacy of another set of norms, while deserters seem to be self-oriented and expressing their own agendas.

Once the members of a group have been rated on each of the four dimensions, their relative positions in the group can be depicted using the same format as the Field Diagram of Bales (see Figure 8.3). However, in this case the forward-backward axis is represented by the serious-expressive dimension. The positive-negative axis remains the same and the upward-downward dimension is again represented by different sized circles. Since each dimension can be represented on a seven-point scale, the two axes of serious-expressive and positive-negative would be divided into seven units, with the number four at the center. The circles would be depicted in seven different sizes, with the smallest circle representing the submissive end of the continuum. The rating on conformity could be indicated by a number, from one to seven, near the dot representing the location of the individual on the plane of the Field Diagram. One could also use other methods of indicating the degree of conformity. For example, the circles for the conformists might be white, the nonconformists black, and persons who are neutral, blue.

However, the degree of conformity is indicated on the diagram, the result would be to highlight the presence of two subgroups within the larger group. One set, given as Types 1-8 in Table 8.2, are the conformists who stand ready to maintain the status quo. The other set, given as Types 9-16 in the table, are the nonconformists who do not support the status quo and are more open to social change, in some cases actively proposing it. Thus, if one were trying to compose a group to work on a well defined task on which all members might be expected to agree, then one would choose persons who could play the roles of Types 1 through 8. On the other hand, if one wanted to open a new frontier or to organize a movement for social change, then one might recruit persons who could play the roles of Types 9 through 16. For maximum creativity all the types are needed; the nonconformists to come up with the new ideas and the conformists to shape them and market them.

Four Perspectives on Roles

When the roles in a group are not fixed, as in an ad hoc laboratory group or in crowd behavior, the four-dimensional scheme is a good one to use for observation. One can look at the behaviors and the images presented to discover how the interactions can flow, sometimes very rapidly, from unification to polarization; how leaders arise; how subgroups form and disband. The dramaturgical approach carries this type of analysis a step further by focusing on the theme carrier and the various parts played to support or counter this theme. Examples of the functions of various types of theme carriers are given in Redl's (1942) descriptions of ten types of central members.

When the roles in a group are relatively well established and the observer is concerned about how well they are played in the interest of the group task, then the AGIL categories would provide a useful starting place for role analysis. Closely associated with this perspective is exchange analysis, in which the focus is on the interaction between persons playing different roles. Through exchange analysis the actual rights and duties of each role can be observed. Social exchange is just another way of looking at the process of social control. In an effort to keep members within the bounds of their roles some things are offered, others are withheld. If the exchange is satisfactory to all parties then we have an instance of conformity. If one party does not concur, we have an instance of nonconformity.

This chapter on roles has included a discussion of leader roles, since the "group atmosphere" that leaders bring with them to a group actually implies a set of roles as one type of behavior "pulls" another (White and Lippitt, 1960). The literature on the communication network can also be subsumed under the concept of role, since the specification of whom is allowed to speak with whom in a group is one aspect of role.

Social Science Adrift

An indication of some of the events surrounding the voyage of the raft *Acali* has been given in Chapter 5 as an example of group development. Although originally conceived of as a peace demonstration, the voyage was described as a floating laboratory for social science at the time of its sailing. This "scientific" side required someone to play the role of scientist, a role in the Adaptive area since it required the collection of information. In terms of the pattern variables (Figure 8.1) the role required a stance that was universalistic and specific.

The role of captain of the crew (goal attainment) required an approach involving affectivity with a concern for performance. The role of family head (integration), in this case the father, called for diffuseness and particularism. The role of founder of the expedition (pattern maintenance) placed an emphasis on quality and neutrality. In effect, the roles of captain and father required a close relationship with crew members, while the roles of scientist and founder required distance.

Although Genovés was clearly the founder of the expedition, he might have chosen not to go along, or if he did go, to play only that role. He had on board a graduate student in anthropology who might have been given the responsibility for data collection, a woman with a license as a merchant marine officer who had been engaged as the ship's captain, and a Catholic priest who already played the role of "father" in another context. However, at various points during the voyage Genovés did try to play the other roles, but found it very difficult because of the incompatible role requirements.

Summary

The most common division of roles that has been identified in groups is between a task specialist (Adaptation and Goal attainment) and a social-emotional specialist (Pattern maintenance and Integration). The activities of leaders and followers in each of the four functional (AGIL) content areas can also be seen as constituting roles. In terms of Parsons's pattern variables the salient characteristics of the Adaptation role are Universalism and Specificity; of the Goal attainment role, Affectivity and Performance; of the Integration role, Diffuseness and Particularism; and of the Pattern Maintenance role, Quality and Neutrality.

Olmsted has suggested a further breakdown within each functional area by considering the extent to which a role is associated with "differentiation" (for example, the "staff" officers in a military organization), or with "integration" (for example, the "line" or command officers). As subroles within each of the broader functional areas, each of these two roles is in the "task" area, with the "staff" function representing the Adaptation subrole and the "line" function representing the Goal attainment subrole.

For the consideration of roles from the point of view of process dimensions, Bales has provided a 26-role typology of combinations of the three dimensions upward-downward, positive-negative, and forward-backward. He has also shown how persons playing these roles can be expected to interact with each other and how the positions of the group members can be plotted on a field diagram. He offers a set of heuristic hypotheses concerning the probable behavior of persons in different positions with respect to the whole group and its subgroups.

A second typology of 16 roles was developed from combinations of behavior on the four dimensions of dominant-submissive, positive-negative, serious-expressive, and conforming-nonconforming. This second set, which incorporates the major features of Bales's analysis, places more emphasis on the extent to which persons stand ready to support the status quo or are more open to social change.

PART III

PROBLEM-SOLVING AND CREATIVITY

The third part concludes the book by considering group problem-solving and creativity, especially for social problems, in the light of the perspectives outlined in Part I with consideration of the aspects of process and structure outlined in Part II. Since an increase in group size is usually associated with an increase in productivity at the expense of member satisfaction, the decision method of consensus is suggested as one way to combine the advantages of both small and large groups.

The final chapter summarizes the literature on individual and group creativity. Mechanisms for stimulating the "creative shift" are indicated for each of the four main levels of creativity. An outline of seven steps involved in the creative problem-solving process is presented in the form of a flow chart.

Chapter 9

Group Size
and Consensus

Group size has been a variable of interest to social-psychologists since the earliest experimental work with groups. In 1898 Triplett set a trend with his study of "the dynamogenic factors in pacemaking and competition." He wondered if having more persons present would affect an individual's performance if the other persons were, or appeared to be, in competition. Other early studies in Germany before 1905 compared the individual schoolchild working alone at home and in the classroom. Taylor, in 1903, observed that laborers in the steel industry in the United States would slow the pace of their work to conform to a group norm if they were working with others rather than alone. Simmel, writing in 1902, was also interested in the differences between a person "alone" and in larger groups, especially the dyad and the triad, which he noted had special characteristics. The dyad provided an intimacy and the possibility of sharing a secret that larger groups lacked and the triad was characterized by a tendency to split into two against one.

Thus the basic questions about group size that continue to interest social-psychologists at the present time were already being posed before 1905: How does an audience or the presence of a group affect individual problem-solving? Are groups more productive than individuals and if so, what is the optimal size of the group? How is the size of the group related to individual conformity to norms, to an individual's opportunities for leadership, or to an individual's pattern of choosing others or being chosen?

AUTHOR'S NOTE: Most of the material in this chapter, with the exception of the description of the laboratory experiment on consensus, is a revision of my article "Group Size," American Behavioral Scientist 24, 5: 695-708. Copyright © 1981 Sage Publications, Inc.

In the 1960s as social-psychologists turned their attention to topics of more current interest (such as helping behavior, bargaining, crowding, and the use of personal space), group size again appeared as a significant variable. In some cases the research was motivated by a public event, such as the murder of a young woman in the presence of a number of bystanders, that led to a series of studies of helping behavior. In other cases the motivation was provided by a new official ruling, as when the U.S. Supreme Court decided that juries of 6 persons could be used instead of the traditional 12-person jury. Since, as Simmel noted, many organizations, such as the military, use group size as a principal basis for organization, it is not surprising that the optimal size of group for any given task should continue to be a subject of interest.

Brief Summary of Research From
1898 Through 1978

Some of the major generalizations resulting from research on the influence of group size from 1898 through 1978 can be summarized briefly as follows (Hare, 1976b: 230-231):

Although the size of the natural group varies with the age and other social characteristics of the population, casual work or play groups most often have only two or three members, while the modal size of an adolescent gang is about ten members. Members are generally less satisfied with the group if the size is increased.

As each additional member joins a group, the number of potential relationships between individuals and subgroups increases rapidly, thus placing more demands on the leader in coordinating group activity. The time available to each member for communication decreases, the gap between the top participator and the other group members grows proportionately greater, and an increased proportion of the members feel threatened and inhibited as size increases.

With the addition of new members, the resources of the group are increased so that a variety of problems may be solved more efficiently; however, after some point, depending upon the task, the addition of new members brings diminishing returns. Although the group may take less time to complete the task, it is less efficient as measured by unit of time per person, and the range of ideas available is increased at the expense of greater difficulty in reaching consensus in the absence of any clear-cut criteria for judgment.

The quality of the interaction process for a group decision changes with increasing group size as groups use more mechanical methods of introducing information, are less sensitive in the exploration of different points of view, and make more direct attempts to reach a solution whether or not all members agree. The interaction pattern in a group of two has unique characteristics that suggest a delicate balance of power in making decisions. Above the size two, there are differences between groups with even and odd numbers of members. Possibly as a result of the fact that the group often splits into two opposing subgroups of equal size, there is more disagreement and antagonism in even-sized groups. Laboratory groups of size three characteristically form a coalition of two, leaving one member isolated; however, the same tendency is not observed in family groups of mother, father, and son. When coalitions do form between members of unequal power, a pair will join forces to maximize their reward and minimize the temptation to form a different coalition.

The optimum size for a small discussion group may be five members, since members are generally less satisfied with smaller or larger groups. In smaller groups members may be forced to be too prominent, and in larger groups they may not have enough opportunities to speak. In the group of five, strict deadlocks can be avoided and members can shift roles swiftly. To select the appropriate size group for a given problem, Thelen (1949) has suggested the "principle of least group size." The group should be just large enough to include individuals with all the relevant skills for the problem's solution. In the use of "Synectics," a form of creative problem-solving developed primarily for business applications, Gordon (1961: 72-73) finds that five persons representing a cross-section of a business firm are enough to provide all the necessary skills and points of view.

If the number of persons in a group is too large for the space it is given to occupy, members are more likely to feel crowded in small rooms where everyone can be seen. Under crowded conditions persons react more negatively to each other. However, in contrast to men, women tend to find smaller rooms more comfortable and intimate. When possible, people will avoid crowded situations.

The research on helping behavior provides additional evidence concerning the influence of different sized groups. Although many studies of helping behavior involve field experiments in which an accomplice drops things in public or appears to be having difficulty changing a flat tire on a lonely road, the basic design is similar to the early experiments recording the influence of the presence of an audience or a group on individual behavior. In this case the focus is not problem-solving behavior but one manifestation of positive behavior, namely helping. In general, the findings from the research on helping behavior are that the larger the number of observers who are not helping someone in need of help, the less likely a subject is to help, especially if the costs for helping are high and the help is not important. As with other tasks, the kind of group involved and its relationship to the subject makes a difference in the likelihood of helping. Thus, the specification of the number of persons present in a group or audience may well tell us something about individual or group behavior "on the average" but the gross effects of size may also be countered by the influence of some other variables with opposite effects on the social system under observation.

Group Size in Relation to the Functional Problems

One way to look at the effects of increasing or decreasing group size is to consider the effects in relation to the four major functional problems of groups. As indicated in Chapter 1, for a group to be successful, the members must be able to handle the problems of pattern maintenance, adaptation, integration, and goal attainment.

The effects of changes in group size are similar to the effects of certain changes in leadership style, communication network, or mode of reaching individual and group goals. Each of these aspects of a group is often considered to be an "independent" variable in reviews of the research literature on group dynamics. Yet in relation to their effects on a group's ability to meet its functional needs, the variables can be seen to be interrelated. If one compares the following:

Large groups vs. small groups
Authoritarian leadership vs. democratic leadership
Centralized (wheel) communication networks vs. decentralized (circle) communication networks
Groups where members are in competition vs. those where members cooperate

the major results are always the same. For large groups, authoritarian leadership, centralized communication networks, and groups in which members are in competition, one finds an increase in productivity coupled with low satisfaction for the average member. (The central person is usually quite satisfied.) Stogdill, in his *Handbook of Leadership* (1974: 413), provides two clues to understanding the relationship between these "variables" in his summary of theory and research on leadership. In relation to group size, he finds two major generalizations concerning leadership; one that "large groups make greater demands on the leader" and the other that in a large group it is "more difficult for a randomly selected member to acquire leadership." Thus the greater demands on the leader in the large group tend to make the person more authoritarian and use a more centralized communication network. The members in turn are in competition for the scarce resources of the group including the attention of the leader and the rewards that come from sharing the leadership position. Although one can vary leadership style, communication network, and mode of reaching individual and group goals without changing the actual size of the group (although the number and nature of the subgroups may vary), one cannot vary group size without having an effect on the other three "variables."

In terms of the four functional problems, an increase in group size (or a comparable change in leadership style, communication network, or mode of interaction) tends to (1) reduce members' feelings of *identity* with the group and *commitment* to its values; (2) provide a greater pool of *skills* and *resources* so that the probability of finding an elegant solution to the problem may be greater although the average member contribution may be less; (3) require a clearer definition of the *norms* and a greater degree of *role differentiation* if the group is to make the best use of its resources, while group *solidarity* is more difficult to maintain; and (4) require more *control* on the part of the leadership to coordinate the role activity of the members as they use the resources to reach the goals that are consistent with the values of the group.

Subgroups

Although it is possible to demonstrate that there are differences in patterns of interaction and in the solutions to functional problems between relatively small groups of five members and larger groups of twelve or thirty members, there are also differences within groups of any given size that indicate that we may not be looking at a single group but rather at a set of subgroups and individuals who happen to occupy the same physical space and have some form of coordination in reaching what may appear to be a common goal. The subgroups and individuals may in fact have different goals, but in laboratory experiments, the experimenter usually assumes that the goals have something to do with the task that has been given to the set of individuals.

Bray, Kerr, and Atkin (1978) make this point in a study in which they observed the work of groups of 2, 3, 6, and 10 university students. They concluded that it was not the actual size of the group that was important but the "functional size." As group size was increased the number of nonparticipators also increased, resulting in a functional group size that was smaller than the actual group size.

Bales et al. (1951) had observed this tendency earlier in their report on channels of communication in small discussion groups. As group size was increased from three to eight members, it was more likely that one or two members would do all of the talking while some members would hardly participate. Although Bales did not say directly that in the larger groups, especially, some members might not actually take part in the decision process, he did call attention to the presence of subgroups that might create a pattern that was different from the "base line" model. "We have also found exceptions," he noted, "when two highly interactive and agreeing members form a subgroup vis-a-vis a third neglected or rejected member" (Bales et al., 1951: 468). As indicated in Chapter 8, in his recent work Bales records that while the actual number of persons participating in a laboratory discussion may remain constant, the "group" may actually be going through cycles in which at one time the members are "polarized" into subgroups and at another time are "unified" into a single group (Bales, Cohen, and Williamson, 1979).

The tendency of the triad to split into two against one has been the most extensively studied, from Simmel's work in 1902 through the present (see for example, Komorita and Chertkoff, 1973). Unfortunately, there are so many possible variations, even with groups of three, that it would be difficult for a single investigator to document the differences in interaction pattern associated with each of the types. The fact that high speed electronic computers with vast memories are available in the 1980s that were not in use in the 1950s and before at least makes this possible. For example, Noma and Smith (1978) have developed a computer program for the analysis of small group sociometric structure that identifies 138 types of triads. For larger groups Lindsay (1976) has examined the possibility of subgroup formation in the light of probability theory. He argues that the largest number of ways in which any size group can divide into subgroups of different sizes (including the individual or "monad") is the most likely variant to occur.

Some evidence of the importance of the analysis of subgroup structure comes from an experiment by Wilder (1977) in which he uses the classic Asch (1955) design for studying the effect of majority opinion on individual judgment. In Asch's experiment (detailed in Chapter 6), he noted that an increase in the size of the majority was associated with increased influence on opinion up to a point, after which the effect leveled off. Wilder's contribution is to lead the naive subject to believe that sometimes the number of persons in opposition are there as individuals and sometimes there as a single group. He finds that it is the greater number of individuals or separate groups that is more persuasive rather than the size of a single group in opposition.

Creating Small Group Processes in Large Groups

Recalling the ways in which large groups differ from small groups in their handling of the four functional problems, is there any way that large groups can maintain their advantage in productivity without the loss of commitment and satisfaction on the part of the average member? Usually in a small group, of five members for example, there is enough time to explore in some depth the opinions and feelings of each member of the group and to take them into consideration when reaching a group decision. But with a group several times as large, say 20 or 30 members, there is a tendency to consider the opinions of only the most vocal and high status members and to use some form of majority decision, sometimes leaving a dissatisfied minority that is nevertheless supposed to remain committed to the group goal.

One decision method that tends to preserve the small group process even in groups of considerable size is that of *consensus*. In contrast to majority vote, a group using consensus attempts to combine the best insights of all members to find a solution that incorporates all points of view. A set of guidelines for using consensus is given below (Hare, 1980b: 141-142). The guidelines are presented as positive and negative aspects of the sequence of phases in group development expressed in terms of functional theory (that is, L-A-I-G . . . L; see Chapter 5).

Although the guidelines can be used by groups in which the leadership functions are shared by all group members, it is helpful to designate two specialized roles. One is a *coordinator*, whose main task is to help the group formulate a consensus for each decision. The other is a *recorder*, who records the consensus on each decision as it is reached and reads it out to the group for their approval or correction. By being clear about the wording of each decision as the group moves along, some misunderstandings are removed that occur with the more usual method of taking minutes of a meeting to be approved at the next meeting of the group. If the usual practice is followed, some group members may have already been acting upon different interpretations of the group decision in the interval between the first meeting and the one at which the minutes of the meeting are approved.

Guidelines for Decisions by Consensus

(1) *Do:* Secure agreement to follow the rules for consensus, that is, look for a solution that incorporates all points of view or is best for the group at this time.

Avoid: A zero-sum solution or using majority vote, averaging, or trading as conflict reduction devices.

(2) *Do:* Give your own opinions on the issue. Approach the task on the basis of logic. Seek out differences of opinion to obtain more facts, especially from low status members.

Avoid: Arguing for your own opinions.

(3) *Do:* Address remarks to the group as a whole. Show concern for each individual opinion.

Avoid: Confrontation and criticism.

(4) *Do:* Although the main function of the group *coordinator* is to help the group formulate a consensus and the main function of the group *recorder* is to record each decision as it is reached, all members should help formulate statements about solutions to which all can agree. Even if there appears to be initial agreement, explore the basis of agreement to make sure there is agreement at a fundamental level.

Avoid: Changing your mind *only* to reach agreement.

(5) *Do:* If consensus is reached, make it clear that each group member is responsible to apply the principle in new situations.

Avoid: Pressing for a solution because the time for the meeting is over. If consensus is not reached, postpone the decision until another meeting and do more homework on the problem.

Consensus Versus Majority Vote:
A Laboratory Experiment

A case study involving a "real-life" group using consensus will be presented at the end of the next chapter on creativity, since the method of consensus is one way to arrive at creative solutions for problems involving human relations. Some of the members of the group described in the case study had had years of experience with the method while others were new to it. Even without experienced members in a group it is possible to gain some of the advantages of consensus with only about five minutes of instruction before a group begins to deliberate.

In the following account of a laboratory experiment, groups of university students were given brief instructions for consensus and their approach to problem-solving was compared with their approach using the familiar method of majority vote (Hare, 1980b). The guidelines for consensus used in the experiment are simpler than those given above. The new guidelines were formulated later to bring together the results of the experiment and the field and laboratory studies noted in the next few paragraphs that precede the description of the actual experiment.

In most of the laboratory studies of small groups using consensus in some form as a rule for decision-making, the focus has been on the outcome of the decision rather than on the process. When consensus has been compared with majority vote or with other decision rules, instructions are usually given to the subjects before the experiment and the outcome is then noted, but the groups are not observed while they are at work nor are the members asked to comment on the differences between the two processes. In the present experiment eight small groups of university students each make two decisions, one using consensus and the other using majority vote. The results confirm some of the characteristics of the consensus method that are expected as a result of studies of community groups and indicate that consensus is favored as a group process.

Although majority vote has seemed to be an essential part of the democratic process for many years, in two recent cases in Africa, both involving the formation of a new constitution, consensus has been used when there has been a fear that militant minorities would not go along with a majority decision even if one could be achieved. The first case was when a constitution for Kenya was formed in 1962 prior to independence in 1963. Before turning over the country to the Kenyans the British government gathered about 120 persons, including representatives of the various factions and their advisors, and flew them to London where they were closeted for about two months while they worked out a constitution using consensus. This agreement held for the first two years of independence without modification while the members of the new government were finding their feet.

The second case occurred in 1975-1976 when a constitutional conference was assembled at the Turnhalle in Windhoek, South West Africa/Namibia. Representatives of various "population groups" under the leadership of Dirk Mudge used consensus because they concluded that if they used majority vote then the minority groups would have "no chance at all" (Hare and von Broembsen, 1979).

The idea of using consensus for political decision-making is not new, but it is usually confined to smaller groups and groups in which there is more homogeneity of opinion. In South Africa, for example, majority vote is used in the parliament, while consensus is used in select committees, party caucuses, and the Prime Minister's cabinet. Although majority vote can be used effectively where the minority is willing to go along with the will of the majority or can be coerced to do so, consensus is used where unity and commitment are important.

Perhaps the longest experience with the use of consensus has been accumulated by the religious group of Quakers who have been using consensus in their business meetings for over 300 years. In a discussion they look for a "sense of the meeting." The process involves a search for a new truth that will encompass the concerns of the individual group members as well as the needs of the group as a whole. A functional analysis of a working party of Quakers using this method (Hare, 1973) indicates that in contrast to the typical voting group which may only make decisions that involve the gathering of new information (adaptation) and the exercise of power (goal-attainment), the consensus method is usually used by a group of persons who have a feeling of affection for each other (integration), and above all it involves agreement on common values (pattern maintenance). Thus the consensus method is very powerful because it involves, in a positive way, all levels of the social system and deals with the complete range of functional needs. These conclusions are similar to the way in which the consensus method is usually described in the social-psychological literature (Scheff, 1967; Dodd and Christopher, 1969; Hare, 1976b: 344-345).

One of the most complete sets of rules for the use of consensus by laboratory groups was developed by Hall and Watson (1970) and adapted by Nemiroff and King (1975). In both experiments some groups of university students were instructed in the use of consensus while others were left to solve the problem in their own way. Before the group sessions the individual members were asked to rate fifteen pieces of equipment in the order of their importance for survival on the moon. The group task was to reach a group decision on the rank order of the same items. In no case was a group actually going to the moon. Thus Hall and Watson observed that for some groups there was more concern with commitment to reach decisions than commitment to the decisions reached. They report that the groups using consensus generally used the information available in the group more effectively and made better decisions 17 percent of the time. Nemiroff and King, with some clarification of the instructions, report a greater difference between instructed and uninstructed groups, with 40 percent more of the instructed groups using consensus producing better decisions. However they also report no differences in subjects' reactions concerning satisfaction with group decisions, satisfaction with self-performance, and perceived group effectiveness.

Method

Eight ad hoc laboratory groups were formed by recruiting university students from sociology classes and through personal contact at the universities of Cape Town and Western Cape. The initial plan called for a comparison between twelve racially mixed, seven-person groups. Half of the groups were to have a majority (five) of whites; the other half a majority of so-called Coloureds. All groups were to be males in the first study. However this plan soon fell away as subjects failed to report for experimental sessions and it was necessary to go ahead with the subjects available. This may reflect the fact that the data were collected in 1976 when the attention of students and others in South Africa was focused on events outside the laboratory. (Many Black schools were closed as a result of student protest.) Eventually eight groups were observed, four including both white and Coloured males, two all Coloured (one of these with males and females), and two of white females. The groups ranged in size from four to twelve. One unanticipated significant variable was age. The modal age for students was about twenty years, with white males being up to a year older than females because of military service. However the major variance was introduced by the presence of the Coloured students, some of whom only complete their university education in middle age. Thus there were several students in their thirties, forties, and fifties.

Before the experimental session subjects were given the short form of the General Survey (Kritzer et al., 1974) with measures of authoritarian conformity, aggression, anxiety, extroversion, and verbal intelligence. Since the verbal intelligence text was only available in English, it was not used with the two groups of Coloured subjects who were tested in a predominately Afrikaans university. For the other tests students could choose tests in either English or Afrikaans. Subjects were also asked a few background questions concerning home language, religion, academic rank, number of friends in the group, and previous experience with group leadership. They were each asked to sign a permission slip giving consent to have information quoted or summarized for publication without revealing their names. All signed. They were given two rands for participation in the experiment.

Each group made one decision using either majority vote or consensus and a second decision using the contrasting method. In each case they were asked to imagine that they were being asked, as a cross-section of student opinion, to advise the student government or one of its committees on some policy decisions. With the exception of the first group that had one slightly different task, all groups were first asked to make a decision about the criteria for distributing funds to campus organizations and a second decision about the criteria for selecting projects for community work by the student health and welfare organization. Although the intention was to have two equal tasks, the white students tended to have more opinions about the functioning of campus clubs while the Coloured students had more opinions about community projects since they were almost entirely located in the Coloured sections of the city.

Although a balanced design was planned in which half of the groups would first make a decision using consensus and half using majority vote, this plan was abandoned once it became clear that the other elements of the ideal "controlled" experiment could not be realized. At that point the remaining groups used majority vote first, followed by consensus. This gave them one group experience under a familiar decision rule (majority vote) before trying out a new decision process. The effect would be to maximize the differences in favor of consensus. Before each group discussion, Edwin de Broize, a graduate student research assistant, called for nominations for a coordinator and recorder for a consensus decision; or a chairman and secretary for a majority vote decision. He then chaired the group while a decision was reached on the leadership for the session, using either consensus or majority vote to reach the leadership decision. Once the group leadership was established, Edwin took no further part in the discussion. After about twenty minutes of discussion for each problem, the groups were asked to bring the discussion to a close and assume that the discussion would continue in another session. All sessions were tape recorded and one group recorded on videotape for demonstration purposes and detailed analysis.

Between the two discussions, group members were given a ten-minute break while they were served soft drinks and snacks. At the end of the experimental period each member received a sheet headed "satisfaction ratings." Members were asked to place a tick on each of four lines to represent their degree of satisfaction with either the group decision process or their own part in the decision process for each of the two decision rules. The lines were marked in increments of 25 from 0 to 100 with the 0 end labeled "unsatisfied" and the 100 end labeled "satisfied." They were told that a mark of "0" would mean that they were not satisfied at all and a mark of "100" would mean that they were very satisfied. Once the ratings were complete, the papers were collected and each member in turn was asked to say why he or she rated majority vote higher than consensus, or whatever the case might be. These comments were also recorded and later subjected to a content analysis.

Before each task, group members were given approximately five minutes of instruction in the discussion method they were to use. Each group knew from the start that the experiment involved a comparison of consensus with majority vote. Each group member received the following set of instructions:

Group decision: Majority vote

(1) Members make proposals in the form of motions. The motions are discussed. Votes are taken. If four out of seven members agree, the vote is carried.
(2) Members try to convince the majority of the value of their proposals.
(3) All remarks are addressed to the chairman (not directly to other group members).
(4) The chairman does not argue for or against any motion. His or her task is to ensure orderly discussion procedures.
(5) The secretary records the majority decisions as they are made.

Group decision: Consensus

(1) Members express opinions on the issue. Issues are discussed until solutions are found which incorporate all points of view or are satisfying to all members.
(2) Members try to formulate solutions which will achieve consensus (all agree).
(3) All remarks are addressed to the group as a whole with the permission of the coordinator (not directly to other group members).

(4)   The coordinator does not argue for or against any solution. He or she helps the group reach consensus by formulating proposals which may be acceptable to all members. (The sense of the meeting.)

(5)   The recorder records proposals which appear to represent consensus and reads them to the group so that group members can confirm agreement or modify the proposals.

Results

Individual scores for the General Survey scales, background variables, participation rank in each discussion, and the four satisfaction scores provided a total of fifteen scores that could be used for quantitative analysis. Correlations were computed between all variables for each of the eight groups separately. The only correlation that had an average that was significantly different from zero (at the .01 level) was that between the rank order of participation in the first session and in the second session (average $r = .56$). Thus participation rank tended to be consistent from one session to the other.

A second analysis was carried out using as inputs the mean scores for each variable for each group (N = 8 groups). Groups with older members were more satisfied with the majority vote decision ($r = .73$, $p < .05$). Average satisfaction with the group decision under majority vote was in turn related to average satisfaction with one's own part in the process under majority decision ($r = .80$, $p < .05$). Looking back over the distribution of ages in the groups we find that in four of the groups the oldest person had been chosen chairman for the discussion using majority vote (age range was 24 to 43 years). In another group the second oldest, a male of 43, was chosen rather than the oldest, a female aged 50. Thus it appears that the majority of the groups chose one of their most experienced members to lead under the majority vote rule and when this was done the group on the average was satisfied with the group decision. The correlation between average age and satisfaction with the group decision under the consensus rule was only .26, far from significant.

As with most rating scales, one can find the usual variations in response set in the subjects' use of the 100-point satisfaction scales. One way of "controlling" for part of this is to note whether the satisfaction for consensus is higher than that for majority vote (or vice versa), regardless of the level of the ratings or the magnitude of the difference between the ratings. For ratings of satisfaction with their own part in the process, 25 of the 59 subjects favored consensus, 10 said they were the same, and 24 favored majority vote. Thus consensus rates essentially the same as majority vote on this score. Considering that this was the first experience with consensus for the subjects, it is perhaps encouraging that consensus rates as high as it does.

For the ratings of satisfaction with the group decision process, the results definitely favor consensus. Of the 59 subjects, 30 favor consensus, 11 give equal ratings, and 18 favor majority vote. If we assume that half of the equal votes would go either way, then the difference between the two proportions of 60 percent (favor consensus) and 40 percent (favor majority vote) is significant at the .01 level. Unfortunately when the subjects were asked after the experiment to give reasons for the difference in their ratings, 6 indicated in their comments a shift in favor of consensus while none indicated a shift in favor of majority opinion. As a result, after discussion 36 subjects favored consensus, 8 rated the two methods equally, and 15 favored majority vote. It would appear that in the postexperiment discussion the subjects may have been responding to majority opinion and perceived experimenter demand. However, the nature of the arguments given to justify the opinions suggest that the expected difference between the two methods has in fact been manifest.

The comments concerning satisfaction with the group decision process made by the subjects during the postexperiment group interviews were transcribed from the tapes and divided into three sets: those favoring majority vote, those favoring consensus, and those judging the two methods about equal. Not everyone made comments, especially in the larger groups of so-called Coloured students. Among those who favored majority vote, some were not clear about the consensus method. More than five minutes of instruction and twenty minutes of experience with the method would clearly be needed if the consensus method were to be used by formal groups. However, most groups should require less than 300 years to perfect the method, as the Quakers have done. Some individuals using the majority vote method argue strongly for and hold on to their minority opinions until the end, preferring to "go down in flames."

Subjects who favor consensus report some of the advantages expected from the functional analysis of the Quaker method provided by Hare (1973a). In terms of the four functional requisites of good group process, subjects report the following:

Adaptation	"Get different views that I hadn't thought of." (More facts are made available for the decision.)
Goal attainment	"Can express and change opinions without being forced." (Decisions not subject to power plays from strong individuals or from the majority.)
Integration	"Feel part of the decision process." "Consensus involves everybody." (Inclusion and solidarity are important.)
Latent pattern maintenance	"More basic level of discussion." (More attention to basic values.)

As a result, as one student observed: "One's point of view can always be woven into the final decision."

The subjects who thought the two methods were about equal saw some advantages with each. For example: "Majority vote is cleaner but consensus is more meaningful" and "Consensus has more scope but would use majority vote if time is limited." One subject reported that the group members were so like minded that the differences did not show.

Discussion

It is not possible to compare the results of this experiment with previous research with regard to the quality of the decisions made using consensus and majority vote; however, the process appears to be similar to that used by other groups (especially the Quakers) using consensus. Given groups of equal size and abilities, equal experience with the discussion methods, and adequate time to find solutions, one would expect the consensus method to result in better quality solutions, with higher overall satisfaction among the members and more commitment to the decisions reached.

Summary

From the period of the earliest laboratory studies in the 1890s through the 1980s, social psychologists have been interested in the effects on an individual's behavior and problem-solving performance of having a number of other persons present as an audience, in competition, or cooperating. When groups of persons are working together, an increase in the number of group members is usually associated with an increase in productivity coupled with lower satisfaction for the average member. In terms of the four functional categories, an increase in group size reduces commitment (L), provides more skills and resources (A), requires more role differentiation while solidarity is harder to maintain (I), and requires more control on the part of leadership (G). The optimal size of a group for a discussion is usually five members. With larger groups the actual work is often done by a small subgroup with other members serving as an audience.

One way to preserve the commitment and solidarity of the small group in a large group that has more resources without using a form of centralized controlling leadership is to use the method of consensus for decision-making rather than majority vote or some form of averaging individual opinions. Guidelines for the use of consensus were presented that have the effect of combining the best insights from all group members in a solution that incorporates all points of view or is accepted by the members as the best solution for the group at that time.

Chapter 10

Creativity

Individuals and groups are continually solving problems. When the solution to the problem is new and original there is evidence that some creative process has taken place. The new creation may range from the application of a special skill or a fairly simple rearrangement of existing materials to an entirely new principle or assumption concerning the nature of reality. Barron (1969: 10) has observed that "great original thoughts . . . not only are the results of creative acts, but they themselves in turn create new conditions of human existence."

Psychologists and others who have been interested in understanding the creative process and the characteristics of the creative person have focused their attention primarily on *science*, because of the high value placed in continuing scientific productivity, and on *education*, in an attempt to identify children with creative potential and to provide special learning situations to enhance their creativity. A third source of information comes from the *industrial area*, where various forms of group problem-solving have been proposed for innovative solutions to industrial problems. In this chapter some of the main themes in the literature will be reviewed and summarized from a functional perspective based on the work of Parsons and a sociometric and dramaturgical perspective based on the work of Moreno.

In brief, the ideas that are drawn from Parsons's functional perspective are that a social system has four basic functional areas: economic (A), political (G), legal (I), and religious (L). Also that there are four basic system levels that should be taken into account in the analysis of social

AUTHOR'S NOTE: The section on the Quaker method of consensus and subsequent analysis are from my article "Group Decision by Consensus: Reaching Unity in the Society of Friends," *Sociological Inquiry* (Publication of Alpha Kappa Delta, International Undergraduate Honor Society in Sociology), 1973, Vol. 43: 75-84.

behavior: biological (A), personality (G), social system (I), and cultural (L) (see Chapter 1).

The main focus of Moreno's work was on creativity. He sought to help individuals become more spontaneous and creative in two ways. One was by composing groups of persons who had chosen each other on a sociometric test (see Chapter 7), and the other by helping them to reach an emotional catharsis and gain new interpersonal insights through psychodrama as a method of group therapy (see Chapter 3).

Creativity as a Form of Behavior

Creativity is a form of behavior. Thus, in common with other forms of behavior, it is subject to the same sets of social influences. However, the persons studying creativity tend to study it in isolation from other forms of behavior and do not state the connection clearly. For example, Taylor (1975: 302) describes five components that must be included in a theory of creativity: person, problem, process, product, and climate. These are the same components that one would want to consider in the analysis of any form of problem-solving. Or again, Getzels (1975: 338) notes that creative behavior is a function of five interactive elements: (1) organismic constitution, (2) personality, (3) social institution, (4) group influence, and (5) cultural values. These are the same as Parsons's four system levels with the "I" level indicated by two aspects of social systems: institutions and group influence.

Stein (1974), whose main focus was on scientific and industrial examples of creativity, describes the stages in the process of creativity as essentially those in the scientific method, namely: (1) preparatory (education), (2) hypothesis formation, (3) testing, and (4) communication of results.

The Creative Person

In the search for potentially creative children and adults, social scientists who have developed psychological tests have looked for the presence of four variables: fluency, flexibility, originality, and elaboration. In a summary of research on the characteristics of productive scientists Barron (1969: 102) finds ten traits that are associated with creativity:

(1) High ego strength and emotional stability.
(2) A strong need for independence and autonomy; self-sufficiency; self-direction.

(3) A high degree of control of impulse.
(4) Superior general intelligence.
(5) A liking for abstract thinking and a drive towards comprehensiveness and elegance in explanation.
(6) High personal dominance and forcefulness of opinion, but a dislike of personally toned controversy.
(7) Rejection of conformity pressures in thinking (although not necessarily in social behavior).
(8) A somewhat distant or detached attitude in interpersonal relations, though not without sensitivity or insight; a preference for dealing with things and abstractions rather than with people.
(9) A special interest in the kind of "wagering" that involves pitting oneself against the unknown, so long as one's own effort can be the deciding factor.
(10) A liking for order, method, and exactness, together with excited interest in the challenge presented by contradictions, exceptions, and apparent disorder.

In sum, the creative person is essentially a nonconformist with the capacity to pursue nonconforming and creative ideas in the face of societal pressures to see things as others have seen them and leave things as others have found them.

Creativity and Conformity

The high point in the process of creativity is the "creative shift" when the individual realizes that there is another way of looking at things. This has been called the "Aha!" effect and was dramatized by Archimedes the Greek geometrician who jumped from his bath with the cry of "eureka" ("I have found it") after the creative shift occurred. Gordon (1961: 132) has observed that the moment of the creative shift is associated with a hedonic response in the form of a pleasurable feeling.

If the new ideas (that is, new for the individual) result from conformity to a group already holding different ideas, then we are dealing with the phenomena of attitude change and conformity to group norms which have been a preoccupation of social scientists for many years. Even without the impetus of the devastating results of conformity in Hitler's Germany or the applications of "thought reform" by the Chinese, the subject of conformity would still be a primary concern of social-psychologists since without conformity to some set of norms there is no basis for coordinated group activity.

In a fairly benign form, the group was advocated to enhance the process of attitude change by Lewin (1943) in his classic research on changing the attitudes of housewives toward the type of meat they were willing to serve their families. The main idea, which continues to be used by practitioners of "organizational development," is that attitudes are "frozen" because of the relationship that an individual has to the group holding the attitudes, that the attitudes must be "unfrozen," and finally that the attitudes must be "refrozen" in relation to a new reference group.

In terms of functional theory, as indicated in Chapter 6, individuals are more likely to conform to the opinions of other group members if they are uncertain about the facts (A), are pressured by a majority or some person of power (G), are concerned that some group may not like them (I), or hold values which support conformity (L). In the various group techniques designed to increase creativity, such as "brainstorming," an attempt is made to reduce pressures to conform at all four AGIL levels and to substitute pressure to be a nonconformist. For example, the four rules for "brainstorming" are (Barron, 1969: 132):

(1) Adverse criticism is taboo.
(2) Freewheeling is welcomed.
(3) Quantity is wanted.
(4) Combination and improvement are sought.

The Creative Shift

The "creative shift" in perception can occur to an individual acting alone or as a member of a group. In either case there is a prior state of conformity to the common perception of things or to common forms of behavior, then a period of "spontaneity" when proactive and reactive behavior becomes more frequent and immediate with considerable variety, then the "creative shift" that takes the form of a new perspective or a new formulation of an idea, then the consolidation of the idea, and finally its transmission and acceptance by others. The advantages of the group are that other members may help "warm up" the individual to the spontaneous and creative state, and that once the creative shift has been verbalized (or acted, painted, or otherwise communicated), other members may take on the remaining tasks of consolidation and transmission so that the new idea may eventually be accepted by others. Stein (1974: 319) has noted the importance of supporters, patrons, or the presence of a "psychegroup" to help with the diffusion of an innovation.

For the creative shift to take place, the boundaries of the old categories of perception must be blurred. Castaneda (1968), in his account of the creativity of the American Indian Don Juan, tells how Don Juan would squint at the hillside in order to find "his place" among the trees and rocks. Only by literally "blurring" his perception of the forms of nature could he "see" them in a new relationship.

If the "old categories" of perception are locked in by strong emotional feelings, then some emotional catharsis will be necessary before new insights can occur. The movement towards an emotional catharsis is fundamental for Moreno's psychodrama therapy (as well as many other forms of therapy or sensitivity training). Hollander (1969) has plotted the course of a psychodrama in the form of a curve that begins at a point of zero spontaneity and creativity, then rises to a maximum as the protagonist in the psychodrama enacts a series of scenes with the help of auxiliaries. Just after the peak of the curve comes the catharsis of emotion followed by new insights as the protagonist works through the problem, possibly trying out new forms of behavior in the closing scenes of the drama. During the period of "working through" and the closing activity of "sharing" similar experiences with the auxiliaries and members of the audience, the creativity of the protagonist returns to its normal level.

Given that an emotional catharsis seems to be necessary for a shift in perceptions about oneself and others where the perceptions are anchored in emotions, is it also necessary to have an emotional catharsis before creating a new work of art or creating a new scientific theory? Since the idea of catharsis is not stressed in the literature on forms of creativity that do not involve therapy, the answer is probably not, or at least not to the same extent.

Mechanisms for Stimulating the Creative Shift

The various mechanisms for stimulating the creative shift are described in the literature on "altered states of consciousness" as well as the literature on creativity. Although the altered state of consciousness may lead only to an increase in spontaneity (a higher level of involvement and a break from stereotyped behavior) and not necessarily to a new and creative response or perception, still there can be no "breakthrough" or "creative shift" without some altered state.

The mechanisms for producing altered states of consciousness can be grouped according to the system level at which they have their primary focus, that is, cultural (L), social system (I), personality (G), or biological (A). One can then hypothesize that, following Parsons's application of the idea of a cybernetic hierarchy, that inputs at higher system levels will have a greater potential for stimulating creativity at a higher level than inputs at the lower system levels. The predicted order, from highest to lowest system level, is L-I-G-A.

System level	*Examples of mechanisms*
L — Cultural	Mystical experiences that emphasize being at one with the universe, oversoul, nature, and so on, for example Yoga and Zen.
I — Social system (group)	Providing a "psychegroup" by rearranging an individual's "social atom" for maximum "tele" (two way empathy).
G — Personality	Forms of therapy (psychoanalysis, psychodrama, hypnosis, and so on) that provide emotional catharsis and encourage new insights about the self and others.
A — Biological	Stimulants that have a direct chemical effect (drugs, alcohol, CO_2, fasting), or more external stimulants (strobe lights, flagellation, rhythmic dancing or singing), or using the natural products of the altered state of dreams.

Since the altered state of consciousness is only one part of the process of creativity, mechanisms that operate principally at the biological level may have an unfortunate side effect in that they may, at least temporarily, leave the individual incapable of testing or communicating the new insights. In a similar way persons in therapy may move about in a "zombie"-like state as they focus on their own problems and for the present be unable to deal effectively with larger system levels. At the other end of the continuum, the person who climbs to the mountain top for a period of contemplation on "the meaning of all this" may well return with a set of tablets on which some original thoughts have been recorded that will create new conditions of human existence.

Levels of Creativity

Much of the early research on creativity did not distinguish different levels of creativity; rather, the focus was on the steps in the process that were common to all forms of creativity and on the characteristics of creative persons. Some, like Maslow (1962: 134-135), did make some basic distinctions, but were more interested in applauding and supporting the creativity in everyday life, such as that found in making a good chicken soup. Maslow distinguished between "primary creativity" such as the improvisation in jazz or childlike paintings and "secondary creativity." For secondary creativity, Maslow (1962: 135) notes: "The voluntary regression into our depths is now terminated, the necessary passivity and receptivity of inspiration of peak-experience must now give way to activity, control, and hard work. A peak experience happens to a person, but a person makes a great product." Maslow gives as examples of secondary creativity bridges, houses, autos, and many scientific experiments which he sees as essentially the consolidation and development of other people's ideas.

For the present analysis, the discussion of levels of creativity given by Taylor (1975: 306-308) provides the best fit with the formulations of Parsons and Moreno. Taylor distinguished a level of spontaneity and four levels of creativity:

(1) Expressive—spontaneity, where originality and quality of the product are unimportant (as in children's drawings).
(2) Technical—involving skill and a new level of proficiency (for example, Stradavari's violin).
(3) Inventive—ingenuity with materials, providing combinations to solve old problems in new ways (examples: Edison's light and Bell's telephone).
(4) Innovative—basic principles are understood so that modification through alternative approaches is possible (example: Jung and Adler elaborate on Freud).
(5) Emergentive—involves the most abstract ideational principles or assumptions underlying a body of art or science. In rare instances there is an emergence of an entirely new principle or assumption (examples: Einstein, Freud, Picasso).

Thus there are four main levels of creativity with a "warm up" level of spontaneity.[1]

The levels of creativity in activity in society at large are in turn similar to the levels of creativity in work as it takes place in small groups. In the category system for the analysis of levels of involvement and creativity given in Chapter 3, the first level of "self-oriented" work is comparable to the "expressive" level of Taylor since it may involve part of the "warm up" to group work or creative activity. The remaining four levels of work (stereotyped, real, involved, and creative) parallel levels 2, 3, 4, and 5 of Taylor.

Mechanisms and Levels

The ideas about the mechanisms at each system level for stimulating creativity can be related to those concerning the levels of creativity to provide the following hypothesis: Individual and group mechanisms (processes) that are used to stimulate creativity are linked to a particular level of creativity. These relationship are summarized in Table 10.1, where the four system levels are indicated in the first column on the left. The

TABLE 10.1   Levels of Systems, Creativity, Mechanisms, and the Range of Effectiveness for Mechanisms

System level	Creativity level	Mechanisms for stimulating creativity	Range of effectiveness (creativity levels)
L – Cultural			
I – Social System	5 – Emergentive	Mysticism, consensus	4 and 5
	4 – Innovative	Scientific method	3 through 5
	3 – Inventive	Brainstorming	2 through 4
	2 – Technical	Skill training	2
G – Personality	1 – Expressive (spontaneous)	Therapy	1
A – Biological		Drugs	Biological through 1

row for the cultural level is left blank since for the present we are focusing primarily on the social system level and the effects on creativity from stimulants from lower levels.

At the bottom of Table 10.1 are the personality and biological system levels. For these levels the mechanisms of therapy and drugs and related processes appear to have as their primary effect an increase in the spontaneity of the individual. In the case of therapies, such as psychodrama, there is also an attempt to produce a "creative shift" of insight after a catharsis has been obtained. However, the creativity is centered at the personality and interpersonal levels rather than at the group or social system level.

Starting with the bottom level of the social system, the mechanisms of skill training would have a limited range of effectiveness since it would only provide a new level of proficiency for creativity at the technical level. Brainstorming and similar techniques such as "creative problem-solving" and "synectics" (Stein, 1975) have a wider range; however they would focus mainly on the inventive level. For example, Parnes, who developed "creative problem-solving," provides a generalized check list of things to do when trying to find a new perspective: (1) put to other uses, (2) adapt, (3) modify, (4) magnify, (5) minify, (6) substitute, (7) rearrange, (8) reverse, and (9) combine (Stein, 1974: 216). Gordon (1961) describes the central process of "synectics" as "joining different and apparently irrelevant segments." He urges people who wish to be creative to use metaphors and analogies and to look at things differently. Although the proponents of these various processes for creative problem-solving might hope that the end result would be creations at the highest level, their actual instructions stress finding combinations to solve old problems in new ways, the inventive level.

In contrast, the scientific method has a wider range since it does provide for the understanding of basic principles and encourages the formulation of new theories. However, much scientific activity is at the inventive, or at best innovative level, where the research provides tests of hypotheses derived from current theory. One hopes for a "breakthrough" of the sort that occurred to Einstein, but most scientists must be content with less.

At the top of the list of mechanisms, primarily for social problems, would be various forms of mystical experience designed to find basic principles that underlie a wide range of behavior. I would also include the process of consensus as it was used by great social innovators such as Gandhi. What Erikson (1969) has identified as "Gandhi's Truth" is essentially a process of finding a wider truth (a wider conception of the way that persons can relate to each other) such that all persons involved will see some profit in the arrangement. At its best, consensus does not involve simply an averaging of opinions in some form of compromise, but a new and creative solution (Chapter 9).

Group Decisions by Consensus

As an example of creative decision-making by a group, the following account describes the process in a group of persons, some of whom had experience with the method of consensus as members of the Society of Friends (Quakers). The account is given as it appeared in *Sociological Inquiry* (Hare, 1973a) except that the brief presentation of functional theory has been omitted. The categories used in the analysis are those given in Chapter 1.

The Sense of the Meeting

Quaker historian Howard Brinton has written several books and pamphlets which describe various aspects of the faith and practice of the Society of Friends (Brinton, 1938; 1943; 1952a; 1952b). One of these was written as a "Guide to Quaker Practice" (1943) to help Quakers in the conduct of their affairs. Although the method of reaching consensus is widely used by Friends in their committees and other decision-making groups, it has been developed primarily for the Monthly Meetings at which the business of the Meeting (church) is conducted. The basic unit of the Society of Friends is the Meeting.

Membership is held in the local Meeting rather than in the Society as a whole. To share common concerns, representatives of local Meetings, called "Monthly Meetings" since they tend to meet for business once a month, meet together in "Quarterly Meetings" four times a year. In turn representatives of Monthly Meetings in an area covered by several Quarterly Meetings, will meet together once a year in a "Yearly Meeting." Finally representatives of meetings in several Yearly Meetings covering even larger geographical areas will meet every five years. In every case the "authority" rests with the local meeting and in fact with the individual member. A decision cannot be handed down from the top. To provide a basis for action a decision must have the consensus of Friends at all levels.

Some of Brinton's suggestions for the conduct of the meeting for business are as follows:*

> Every meeting should hold a business session at least once a month. This should be preceded by a time of worship in order that the spirit of worship may pervade the transaction of business. In both the meeting for worship and the meeting for business, guidance is sought from the Spirit of Truth and Life by whose operation the group is brought into love and unity. . . . Quakerism is not anarchistic. The principle of corporate guidance, according to which the Spirit can inspire the group as a whole, is central. Since there is but one Truth, its Spirit, if followed will produce unity. . . . In the transaction of business the meeting assumes that it will be able to act as a unit. No vote is ever taken. If unity cannot be reached, the meeting does not act. The only necessary official is a clerk whose business it is to apprehend and record the decision of the meeting [Brinton, 1943: 33-36].

> On routine affairs little or no discussion may be necessary, and the clerk may assume that silence gives consent. In such matters the clerk may prepare his minute before the meeting begins, but it must in any case be read and approved in the course of the meeting. On matters which require it, time should be allowed for members to deliberate and to express themselves fully. A variety of opinions may be voiced until someone arises and states an opinion which meets with general approval. This agreement is signified by the utterance of such expressions as "I agree," "I approve," "That Friend speaks my mind." If a few are still unconvinced they may nevertheless remain silent or withdraw their objections in order that this item of business may be completed, but if they remain strongly convinced of the validity of their opinion and state that they are not able to withdraw the objection, the clerk generally feels unable to make a minute. In gathering the sense of the meeting the clerk must take into consideration that some Friends have more wisdom and experience than others and their conviction should therefore carry greater weight. The opposition of such Friends cannot, as a rule, be disregarded. Chronic objectors must be dealt with considerately, even though their opinions may carry little weight.

*From *Guide to Quaker Practice* by Howard H. Brinton, Pendle Hill Pamphlet 20 (Wallingford, PA, 1943), pp. 35-36. Reprinted by permission.

If a strong difference of opinion exists on a matter on which a decision cannot be postponed, the subject may be referred to a small special committee with power to act, or to a standing committee of the meeting. Often an urgent appeal by the clerk or by some other Friend to obstructive persons will cause them to withdraw their objections. It must be remembered, however, that minorities are sometimes right. When a serious state of disunity exists and feelings become aroused, the clerk or some other Friend may ask that the meeting sit for a time in silence in the spirit of worship. The effect of this quiet waiting is often powerful in creating unity [Brinton, 1943: 36-38].

(Note that the meeting for worship [religious service] among Friends consists of a group of people sitting in silence until someone is moved to give a message to the group. After each message, there is again silence while the message is considered. Thus a call for "a few minutes of silence" in a business meeting emphasizes the fact that the business meeting is also a religious meeting at which business is being conducted. It serves to remind Friends that each individual opinion should be considered thoughtfully and that truth is to be sought.)

To succeed fully the members should be bound together by friendship, affection and sympathetic understanding. Factions and chronic differences are serious obstacles. The members should be religiously minded, religion being a powerful solvent of the type of self-centeredness which makes group action difficult. . . . The attitude of a debater is out of place. The object is to explore as well as convince. . . . Friends' method of attaining results exhibits principles typical of organic growth. The synthesis of a variety of elements is often obtained by a kind of cross-fertilization, and the final result is not therefore, or at least ought not to be, a compromise. Given time and the proper conditions, a group idea, which is not the arithmetical sum of individual contributions nor their greatest common devisor but a new creation or mutation, finally evolves. . . . Each speaker credits every other speaker with at least some genuine insight. Thus the united judgment is slowly built up until it finds such expression by some individual as can be endorsed by the meeting as a whole. No minority should remain with a feeling of having been overridden [Brinton, 1943: 40-41].

Another view of the method of consensus is given by Hallock Hoffman in a paper on "The Quaker Dialogue," part of a publication on *The Civilization of the Dialogue* from the Center for the Study of Democratic Institutions. It is Hoffman (1968: 10) who makes the distinction between "unity" and "unanimity."

Unity, not unanimity, is the aim of the meeting. The distinction is crucial. A group organized according to the rule "one man, one vote" reaches unanimity, that special condition of majority rule in which the majority happens to include all the members. Unity is more complex. It does not necessarily reflect total agreement on the issue under discussion. It incorporates a perception of the relationship of the members to each other and to the issue. . . . The unity sought is a recognition of what decision is proper for the meeting as a whole. Unanimity requires that all reach the same opinion on the issue to be decided. Unity requires all to reach the same conclusion about what should be done in the name of all, even when opinions may still differ.

Hoffman (1968: 12) also sees the method of consensus as part of the Quakers' nonviolent approach:

> Nonviolence means more than non-killing; it means respect, even reverence. It means caring enough about each member of society to renounce *any* action that will violate him, even if the violation is only to his spirit.

Other authors have noted additional aspects of the relationship between the individual and authority in the use of the consensus method:

> The most rebellious soul can joyfully accept a discipline which respects him so completely as an individual. Conversely, the Quaker can afford his freedom, *because* he is strengthened by a profound union, ever renewed in the life of the Meeting [Pollard, Pollard and Pollard, 1949: 50-51].

In finding a solution to a problem before a business meeting:

> The issue was not compromised but moved up to another level where a new plan was evolved—a plan in nobody's mind at the beginning of the discussion [Chase, 1951: 49].

In work camps organized by the American Friends Service Committee the business meetings procedure is used. There is a danger if the director of the camp acts as the clerk:

> This situation then presents a considerable opportunity for authoritarian elements to enter and disrupt the democratic pattern, and places a heavy burden upon the director to maintain a genuinely democratic group discussion and to arrive at consensuses that accurately reflect the positive wishes of the group and not merely deference to the director in his role as 'clerk' [Riecken, 1952: 59].

Additional references to the conduct of the Quaker business meeting are to be found in the books of *Faith and Practice* published by each Yearly Meeting. These books contain examples of Friends' practice in the past and questions to guide Friends in the future. There is no creed and no single set of beliefs which must be endorsed by all Friends. Thus the actual conduct of Friends' business procedures is free to grow and develop in keeping with contemporary group practice. This, as we shall see in the case cited below, can even include current techniques from "sensitivity training." Still the basic principle of unity has remained for over three centuries.

A Case Study:
The 1970 Working Party

In 1969 the Philadelphia Yearly Meeting, composed of representatives of the Monthly Meetings in the Philadelphia area, faced a difficult decision. A group of militant blacks had presented the Yearly Meeting with a "manifesto" demanding that a considerable sum of money be turned over to a black development company as "reparations" for the wrongs suffered by members of the black community in times past. Because of the controversial nature of the issue a committee of 16 persons was formed to draft a response to the black manifesto. When this document was presented at Yearly Meeting it was evident that the meeting was far from unity. The 16-person committee, which contained no blacks, asked that it be "laid down" (disbanded). However, some further attempt needed to be made to reach consensus on the issues so that a new committee of 38 members was formed, containing both whites and blacks. (And also both men and women since the separate meetings for men and women had been joined in the Society of Friends many years ago.)

The primary data for this case study consist of the minutes of 25 meetings of this committee, called the 1970 Working Party, during the period April 1970 through May 1971, and other documents provided by the Clerk of the Working Party for that period. In July 1971 the Clerk was interviewed to establish the main turning points in the development of the group and to bring out points which were not evident in the minutes. In May of 1971 the first Clerk resigned and a second Clerk was appointed to fill his place. With some changes in membership, the Working Party was to continue through 1971-1972.

The actual work of the Working Party over the 12-month period was to produce a "preliminary report" which consisted of a preamble and two parts. Part One was a proposal for a process which would allow Friends at the Monthly Meeting level to "look to their possessions, practices, and relationships, 'to try whether the seeds' of exploitation and oppression lie in them." Part Two was a suggestion that an Economic Development Fund for Disadvantaged Minority Groups be established with a Board of Managers, initially drawn from the Yearly Meeting but within a three-year period turned over to representatives of minority groups. Although a Development Fund had been proposed by the first committee, the form of the "preliminary report" was something which grew out of the Working Party's attempts to reach consensus on the issues. Without going into much more detail of the *content* of the issues we will now try to follow the group *process* as the members worked towards consensus.

Following a procedure used in earlier case studies (Hare, 1968), the one-year period was divided into shorter "natural" time periods. The beginning of a new time period is generally marked by a change in membership, leadership, or group activity. In this case the year period could be divided into four phases as follows:

Phase	Months	Number of Meetings	Highlights of Process
1	April-June 1970	5	Working Party meets to "look for will of God." A member of the Yearly Meeting staff makes suggestions. Two Friends leave over four-letter words.
2	3 days in June 1970	1	At a weekend at a Quaker religious study center, members come to know each other and subcommittees begin work on report.
3	July-November 1970	10	Agenda lists many tasks. Many disagreements are recorded. Part One of report is presented to Representative Meeting for approval.
4	December 1970 to May 1971	9	Subcommittees present panel discussions of problems raised by report at Quarterly Meetings. Part Two of report is presented to Representative Meeting and later the entire report is presented to Yearly Meeting. The first clerk resigns.

To give some further indication of the content and process during each phase we will consider some selected quotations from the minutes and comments by the clerk.

Phase 1—At the first meeting of the Working Party there was a concern expressed about the composition of the committee and its purposes. This was recorded in the minutes as follows: "There was a question raised as to whether the appointed membership should be confined to members of the Yearly Meeting. (A member of the Yearly Meeting staff) stated that he had had a letter concerning this question also. He had answered saying that he thought it was the sense of the

Yearly Meeting that this Working Party was looking for the will of God, and not necessarily the will of Friends. . . . It is important to have all the help and knowledge possible from members and individuals closely associated with Friends" (4/15/70).

Several committee meetings later this same member of the Yearly Meeting staff suggested that the committee discontinue looking for some corporate action they could agree upon since they seemed so far from unity. Instead he suggested that Friends produce a series of "position papers" on subjects such as racism, ecology, population control, morality, public education, Friends' education, Friends' institutions, investments, property, privilege, war, national priorities, housing, and violence. These suggestions were not followed but do show the concern that the committee be given a definite set of tasks since some members felt that the committee lacked direction at this point.

An example of the tensions which became manifest from time to time and the way Friends reacted to them is found in the minutes of 5/14/70:

> Early in our meetings, the group and individuals had to labor with anger and tension caused by the use of "gut language" four-letter words expressed and objected to. In the heated discussion both (X) and (Y) left our meeting. In defense of "four-letter words" it was noted that these may be used by the young to elicit response, although others felt this was not so. Compared to what is going on in the world these are not obscenities to the young. We must recognize that this is the language of the ghetto, and that we should not pin our middle-aged and middle class "hangups" on others. Some feel that this is a generation difference; others that it is an experience difference. "Four-letter words" are not as painful to some as veiled unkindnesses such as "non-Friend" politely said. On the other hand, it seems unkind to continue such expressions when we know that it hurts others; a lack of "caring" is indicated. We all come from different experiences; it is hoped that we can develop a warm relationship and be sensitive to each other's differences.

> It was pointed out that we need to keep to the central point, which is Christ. We are working to be helpful and constructive; the revolution envisioned by the young may not lead to a "brave new world" but to dictatorship and repression. It was said that in our Meeting next time we should keep in mind the things which we should be changing now. Our young people are leaving the Society of Friends, and we should be doing more and be helping to say "no" to this "rotten" society. In rebuttal, it was said that we and our young people should have a commitment to work for change, that leaving us is giving up, and that no matter how many times we have been over this ground we have to keep on working. It was earnestly hoped that both (X) and (Y) will return to our meetings.

The clerk of the Working Party summarized this first phase by noting that the committee was new to the issues. They were getting the issues out and trying to find their direction. In the first five weeks there were some real points of tension. Some of the discussions were hot and heavy. When the member of the Yearly Meeting staff saw the group floundering with the new ideas and the new terminology he offered some suggestions in writing as a way of dealing more systematically with the issues. However his suggestion for a series of "position papers" was not taken up because some members felt that the group was dealing with their own subconscious attitudes and that the only way to come to grips with them was through personal, free-flowing confrontation. At this time the clerk said that he felt as confused as everyone else since he had not resolved the questions in his own mind. He did not feel that he could lead and as a result was very permissive. Later he did try to exercise leadership when he sent out an agenda for the special long weekend meeting in which he tried to state the issues to be resolved.

Phase 2—The long weekend meeting at a Quaker religious study center was a phase in itself. The preamble to the report was written there and subcommittees were formed to work on Parts One and Two. The clerk recalls that the weekend started off with some "sensitivity training" techniques of self-revelation and communication. Going around the circle, each member was asked in turn to recount incidents where he had acted in a racist fashion. Members also gave examples of institutional racism. There was a dissertation by one of the black members on black separatism. On Saturday night they had a party. Several persons stayed up late and kept at the discussion. There was a great sense of comradeship. At the end there was a self-congratulatory session since members felt they had grown and changed.

The minutes of the next meeting record that the weekend "had been very successful." Several members "spoke about how much they appreciated the opportunity, and how much they felt had been accomplished in terms of the group getting to know themselves better, and to struggle with the matter of coming up with a workable plan for the Yearly Meeting" (7/9/70).

Phase 3—This phase was a major period of work for the group. For one meeting during this period the agenda lists nine tasks for the group to consider (7/30/70). However, arriving at consensus was not easy. Some minutes seem to record more points of disagreement than agreement. For example, the minutes of 8/20/70 state:

It soon became apparent that there was a wide divergence of view as to the composition of the "Board of Directors," which by common consent was changed to be the "Board of *Managers.*" Some felt very strongly that this Board of Managers should be entirely composed of Quakers. Others felt equally strongly that to have all, or even some, Quakers on the Board would be to violate the principle of self-determination which was stressed in the Preamble. The Working Party labored long and hard over this issue, but at the conclusion of the Meeting the spread of view appeared to be as wide as ever.

The phase ended when the Preamble and Part One of the report were presented to Representative Meeting for approval. The Representative Meeting is a smaller Meeting of Friends which meets monthly to act for the Philadelphia Yearly Meeting in the interval between the Yearly Meetings. An initial presentation was made one month and a second presentation made a month later. The second meeting was preceded by a long period of worship, a recognition of the sensitivity of the issues. The Working Party minutes record:

> The members of the Working Party who were present at Representative Meeting reported on this meeting. They expressed how different in tone this meeting was compared to the one the month previous when the report was initially presented. The opportunity for people to consider it for an additional month was helpful. The long period of worship prior to the discussion of the Working Party report at this meeting of the Representative Meeting was a very moving experience (12/10/70).

Phase 4—During the fourth phase subcommittees of the Working Party presented panel discussions at the various Quarterly Meetings in the area. The panels discussed the issues facing the Yearly Meeting and stressed the need for a continuing search for social justice. As before, the religious nature of the work is emphasized. In a letter to members of the Working Party from the clerk giving suggestions for organizing the panel discussions, the closing sentences are: "At least two hours should be given to the program which should be conducted in the spirit of worship. There should be ample time for dialogue, first among the panelists and second among the Friends present, as they search for truth along with the panelists" (Memo, 1/7/71). The phase closed as Part Two of the report was presented to the Representative Meeting and the entire report presented to the Yearly Meeting.

During this phase there was considerable role differentiation with a Chairman appointed for the subcommittee to prepare the presentations for the Quarterly Meetings and another Chairman for the subcommittee to prepare the presentation for the Yearly Meeting. The Clerk noted that the group was able to work very quickly during this phase since the members had already worked through so many things together. At the end of the year the first Clerk resigned and a new Clerk was appointed.

Analysis

The first step in the analysis of the case material presented above will be to note those aspects of the Friends' method of reaching consensus which are common to all problem-solving groups. The second step will be to note the ways in which this method differs from formal or informal methods of taking a majority decision.

In general the Working Party developed as a group in the expected sequence of L-A-I-G. The first phase combined pattern maintenance (L) and adaptation (A). The problem of defining the basic purpose of the group was reflected in the concern about the composition of the committee. A group is often in a very dependent state during this period, with members turning toward the leader for direction. In this case, since the formal leader, the Clerk, was not providing strong leadership, the staff member from the Yearly Meeting felt that he should come forward to offer guidance for the group.

Since the membership of the Working Party was composed to represent a cross-section of Quaker opinion, the group needed information about this opinion in order to make decisions later. Thus we see the members working, in the area of adaptation (A) by sounding each other out in the "hot and heavy" discussions.

Once a group has the resources it needs, some integrative experience is usually needed to provide a high level of morale so that the group can carry through with the task. Also roles appropriate for the task should be defined. For the Working Party the long weekend provided the necessary integration (I). The members report a high point in morale. They also begin the first real work in the goal attainment area (G) as the subcommittees are formed to work on Parts One and Two.

By Phase 3 the Working Party has definitely entered the goal-attainment area. This is marked by considerable differentiation in function. Having come to grips with the issues themselves, the committee members now go out as panels to make presentations to the Quarterly Meetings. The success of these panel discussions (G) feeds back to the pattern-maintenance area (L) since it gives the group an increased sense of its worth and its ability. However it is not a major change in L since the basic composition of the committee has not changed. In contrast to the success in goal-attainment which has a positive effect on L, the loss of group members from time to time has a negative effect on L since it raises doubts about the value of the group and its ability to reach consensus.

Phase 4 represented a second period of goal-attainment at a higher level of differentiation and productivity. By this time the committee has done everything once. In Phase 2 they have successfully presented part of their report to the Representative Meeting and they have faced the Quarterly Meetings. Now they go through similar steps as they prepare for the final presentation to the Yearly Meeting. Although their meetings are still not conflict free, they have become a skilled problem-solving team.

The method of reaching consensus differs from other ways of taking majority decisions in that it emphasizes the integrative and pattern-maintenance areas rather than simply the adaptive or goal attainment areas. The simplest decisions are ones which involve only the adaptive area. When a judgment is to be made about the facts, especially when "the facts speak for themselves," members of a group may reach unanimity because they all see things in the same way. These decisions are also the easiest to change because a new set of evidence will lead to a new decision. More lasting are decisions reached because the group leader (or a majority) has the power to coerce members into compliance with a group decision (goal-attainment area). As the Asch (1955) experiments have demonstrated, the power of a majority giving a different opinion is enough to influence an individual to agree with a decision which goes against the "facts" as he sees them. However, once the power of the authority or the majority has been removed, the individual may no longer conform. Most voting decisions are of this type. The majority rules as long as it has the power to back up its views.

Moving up the cybernetic hierarchy of control, the integrative area is more effective in producing conformity than the goal-attainment area. If a person conforms to group norms because he likes the other members of the group and wishes to remain their friend, he may hold on to a group opinion even though the group of friends is not actually present but only serves as a reference group. Finally, conformity is most difficult to change if the actor defines the issue as one which involves basic values which represent his whole way of life (pattern maintenance).

In the typical Monthly Meeting where the method of consensus is used, the Friends are also friends, so that integrative pressures come into play. However, the predominant characteristic of the decisions is their religious context. Each decision is seen as a reflection of a basic value position for the members of the group. For Friends, every day is a "holy" day so that every action should be guided by one's fundamental beliefs. Because these beliefs are not taken lightly, they are changed very slowly, only when all agree and the agreement is so evident that a simple "clerk" can record the new sense of truth. Once the decision is reached, each individual is committed to follow this guideline. Further, he is free to act in a very individualistic manner (judged by the standards of society as a whole), safe in the knowledge that he has taken part in the interpretation of the values of his group, of the truth as it has been revealed in the present day. However, the Friend also knows that truth is not fixed and that a continuing re-evaluation of one's value position is required.

Although the Friends continually use "religious" terms in describing their value system, the important part of the distinction from the point of view of functional theory is that the method of consensus involves a decision at the level of values (not necessarily religious values). Further, the consensus method recognizes that the ultimate locus of a set of beliefs and the ultimate unit of action is the individual, so that the most effective decision method is one which leaves the decision firmly anchored in the individual consciousness. Recognizing also that the most effective social control is self-control, the Friends leave it primarily to the individual to modify his own behavior, relatively free from external restraints. Their trust in his judgment and his allegiance to truth is reflected in their view that "there is something of God (truth) in every man."

Summary of Case Study

For over 300 years Quakers have been making group decisions by a method of consensus in which they look for the "sense of the meeting." This process involves the search for a new truth which will encompass the concerns of the individual group members as well as the needs of the group as a whole.

The minutes of a Working Party of Friends over a period of one year are used as a case study of this process. The group, which is struggling with a sensitive social issue, develops through the stages of pattern maintenance, adaptation, integration, and goal-attainment. As the group grows older the members' roles become more differentiated and the members become more skilled at the task.

In contrast to the typical voting group which may only make decisions which involve the gathering of new information (adaptation) and the exercise of power (goal-attainment), the consensus method is usually used by a group of members who have a feeling of affection for each other (integration), and above all it involves agreement on common values (pattern maintenance). Thus the consensus method is very powerful because it involves all levels of the social system and deals with the complete range of functional needs.

A Flow Chart for Group Creativity

To provide a summary and integration of the ideas about group creativity that have been presented in this book I conclude with a "flow chart," as one would for a computer program, indicating in outline the steps that may be involved in the creative process, together with some details of the activities for each of the steps. We should note once more that the problem-solving steps would be the same for an individual who is trying to find a creative solution. However, at least with social problems, it is better if the individual involves others in the process at every point at which it is possible. There may be times when you are the only one who seems to understand that there is a problem or the only one who seems to be searching for a solution. In that case, I urge you to follow your "concern" even though the road leading to a solution may be a lonely one for a while. Others may be on the road just ahead or may be waiting to follow once you have shown the way.

The major steps in the creative process are shown in Figure 10.1 in flow chart form. The first step in the creative sequence is to define the problem

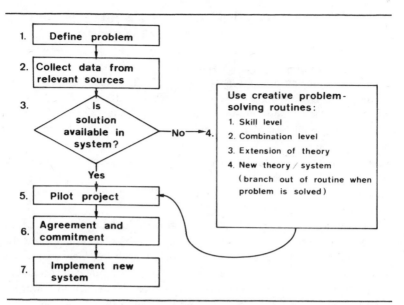

Figure 10.1 Steps in the Creative Process

that requires a creative solution. In some cases the problem may be presented by some other individual or group, as it was for the Quakers who faced the problem of "Black reparations." In other cases the realization that there is a problem may result from something that happens to you personally, as it did to Gandhi when he was thrown out of his first class train compartment on his first visit to South Africa. Or the problem may grow out of practical or theoretical concerns of an individual or group.

The second step is to collect data concerning the problem from relevant sources. Although groups may be able to provide solutions to all sorts of problems, they are probably most effective in the solution of social problems where the characteristics of the observer (such as age, sex, social class, ethnic group) have more to do with the collection of data than in the solution of physical or environmental problems. That is, with a social problem, the members of the group can use the diversity of their own backgrounds to provide leads concerning the importance of different types of data as well as to facilitate communication with persons of similar backgrounds who may be important sources of information. For example, in some cultures people under 30 years old find it easier to relate to others who are under 30, or women prefer to talk to women, or persons of ethnic minorities may only feel they can trust someone of their own background.

Thus, for the second and subsequent steps, it is best to compose a team of persons following Thelen's (1949) "principle of least group size" that is relatively small and yet contains persons who will be able to make contact with all sectors of the social system that have an interest in solving the problem or are important for its solution. In the case of Curacao (Hare, Carney, and Ovsiew, 1977), this meant a team of old and young, men and women, and Black and White with relevant social science and action skills. The team should also clearly indicate the kind of value framework in which you hope the solution will be found. In the sensitive political situation on Cyprus, the commitment to a nonviolent solution to the tension between Greeks and Turks was exemplified by including a leader of the Gandhian Movement from India as part of the first fact-finding team (Hare and Wilkinson, 1977).

In addition to obtaining the basic demographic data about each sector of the social system, one can also interview representatives of each sector to record their ideas about the nature of the problem, their own aspirations concerning a solution, their perceptions of the others involved, and their accounts of factors that seem to be blocking movement towards a solution. With this information in hand one can write a "position paper" outlining the views of each sector in turn. The papers for each sector should be checked in draft form with representatives of each sector to ensure their accuracy. If there is a conflict between groups these statements may be polemic in nature. The importance of writing down the opinions at this stage is so that each side knows that you understand their position. Once this has been done the papers can be filed or perhaps circulated without comment to all groups involved. The statements are unlikely to provide a basis for a solution to the problem since they will not yet contain all the facts that will be necessary. It is probable that each side, especially if they have had legal training, will not have included any information that is totally false, but they will probably have stressed things that are true and will support the position of their side.

It is possible for a relatively small team to accumulate more information about a problem than any of the parties involved for several reasons. First, as a "third party" the team will have access to information from all sides, whereas each side is usually limited to information about its own affairs. Second, a specialized team may have more time to devote to the problem than members or leaders in a community who have other day-to-day problems to attend to, and third, the team may include specialists who have not been previously available to work on the problem. For example, on Cyprus, with all of the resources of the United Nations available to find a solution to the tension between Greeks and Turks, one might have thought that a small group could add little. Yet for all the 3000 men in the

United Nations force on Cyprus at any one time, only seven were involved in work with communities and only two in political negotiations (Hare, 1977: 284).

Once the team is clear about all aspects of the problem, it is time to move on to Step 3 to see if a solution is already available in the system or can be borrowed from another system. As Schmuck, Runkel, and Langmeyer (1971: 185) have observed, there may already be some person or some group within the system that has a solution to the problem. Because the person with the solution is considered deviant, of low status, or is outside the central communication network, or whatever, the solution may not have been utilized by the group. In such a case the team only has to facilitate the acceptance of the idea by moving on to Steps 5, 6, and 7.

In a similar way the idea may come from another system or another culture and can be adapted for the present situation. In such a case the experience of agents of change from Lewin (1943) to the present is that we must pay attention to the "gate keepers," those persons who tend to influence the acceptance or rejection of new ideas by a group. It is easier to suggest a solution that is known to have been a success in another situation, as was the case with the achievement motivation approach used on Curacao after the riot in 1969 (Berlew and LeClere, 1974). Again if the borrowed solution seems adequate, go on to Steps 5, 6, and 7.

If no solution can be found inside the system or can be borrowed from another system, then we proceed to Step 4 which is a "package" of problem-solving subroutines for different levels of creativity. One tries to find a solution at the lowest level (skill level) and if that fails, then one moves on to higher levels in turn. Whenever the problem is solved, one branches out of the subroutine package and continues with Steps 5, 6, and 7. That is, if there is no solution at the skill level or if this level is inappropriate, then one tries the combination level. If a combination of older forms does not work, then one tries for an extension of existing theory or cultural forms or laws that might apply in the new situation. If that fails, one tries for a new understanding of basic principles in the form of a new theory or a new system.

As a central part of the process some "creative shift" will be necessary at all levels. At the skill level the relationship to an object or a person may remain but the *form* will have changed, and must be seen to have changed, for example, in acquiring new sensitivity to the feelings of others through "sensitivity training." For a new combination one can use the old perception of the forms but needs a new perception of their *relationships*. For an extension of theory one needs to redefine some action as an instance of the application of a theory or to give a different valuation to existing relationships. Thus some changes in ideas about *both* forms and relationships are required. Finally a new theory requires some new forms (units) and new relationships—as in Guilford's (1975: 39) creativity level of "implications" which involves the redefinition of units.

As I have noted earlier in this chapter, there are mechanisms that can be used by groups (and individuals) to stimulate creativity at each of the levels included in Step 4. For an increase in social or technical skills (technical level) that may produce a more effective system, the "workshop" approach is often used. Persons who are judged to need skill training join with experts for a few hours, or days, or weeks, depending on the nature of the skill, to learn the new skills and to practice them on simulated problems. In the case of learning skills in interpersonal relations, the workshop group itself is often the focus of attention.

"Brainstorming," "creative problem-solving," and "synectics" and similar methods (Stein, 1974, 1975) can be used to find creative solutions, primarily for physical problems, at the level of combinations (inventive) and the level of extension of theory (innovative). However their main emphasis is on finding new combinations of objects by "joining together apparently irrelevant segments" (Gordon, 1961). If the problem is social rather than physical, then one is assuming at the second (inventive) level that the persons involved have the necessary social skills, but that some reorganization or extension of these skills is required; or perhaps it is necessary to compose groups or sets of people with all the required skills to realize the solution.

When the problem requires creativity at level 3, the extension of theory (innovative) or level 4, the development of a new theory or system (emergentive) then the scientific method provides the best developed method for physical problems and the method of consensus is the most sensitive for social problems. To extend a current theory to include the case in hand, one searches through available theories in physical or social science or looks for precedents in religion, law, politics, or economic practice. For this purpose one often consults a panel of experts who are familiar with the various theories that might have some application.

For the development of a new theory or a new form of social organization the steps involved in the scientific method as it applies to physical or social phenomena are set out in many methodology texts. The four stages in the method, as they have been summarized by Stein (1974) are: (1) preparatory, (2) hypothesis formation, (3) testing, and (4) communication of results. Some guidelines for the use of the consensus method have been presented earlier in Chapter 9. The goal of the consensus method is to design a "non-zero-sum" game in which all players can see some benefit. This new system or form of relationship is not necessarily what can be true today, but what might be true if people behaved differently. Finding a solution by consensus may take some time, as in the case of the Quakers and the reparations. However, developing a new theory in physical science can also take some time.

To facilitate the "creative shift" at all levels of creativity and especially the fourth, it is well to allow time for individual withdrawal between the periods of intense group activity (or work on the problem if only one individual is involved). The individual withdrawal could be to connect with the "outside" through the solitary contemplation of the natural surroundings, or to connect with the "inside" though hot baths or other methods of inducing "dream-like" states without the debilitating effects of drugs. One's natural dream states at night should also be analyzed for potential solutions.

If the problem-solving routines in Step 4 yield more than one solution, you may wish to try more than one pilot project and then include the ultimate decision about the "elegant" solution as part of the process of securing agreement and commitment from the people involved in Step 6. If enough individuals or groups are available for the creative effort, you may wish to have someone search for a solution at each of the four levels and then select the most appropriate solution on the basis of some cost-benefit analysis. In any event, once a solution is in hand one is ready to proceed with the final three steps of the pilot project, securing agreement and commitment, and implementing the new system. Each of these steps will be facilitated if key people from the community have been involved in the project from the beginning.

This book, and especially this last chapter, has been a summary of the experience thus far with individual and group creativity. If the methods work, persons using the methods should be able to raise themselves by their own bootstraps; that is, the methods should lead to the creation of even more creative methods. The preparation for the ultimate "breakthrough" is continuous. To quote Fromm (1959: 54): "Education for creativity is nothing short of education for living." To this must be added courage and faith, as Fromm (1959: 54) reminds us:

> To be certain of the reality of one's own experience in thought and in feeling, to be able to trust it, to rely on it, this is faith. . . . Without courage and faith creativity is impossible.

Summary

An act of creativity is a form of behavior that is subject to the same influences from different levels of the social system as any other type of behavior. The stages in the process of creativity are essentially those in the scientific method, namely: (1) preparatory (education), (2) hypothesis formation, (3) testing, and (4) communication of results.

The creative person is autonomous, intelligent, likes abstract thinking, and is challenged by what appear to be contradictions, exceptions, or disorder. On psychological tests the person ranks high on fluency, flexibility, originality, and elaboration.

An essential part of the creative process is the "creative shift" in perception that takes the form of a new perspective on a problem as a person breaks away from a prior state of conformity to older perceptions or understandings. The creative shift can be facilitated by mechanisms that have a primary focus at one of the four system levels; for example, drugs at the biological level, therapy at the personality level, psychegroups at the social system level, and mystical experiences at the cultural level.

Taylor has identified a level of spontaneity and four levels of creativity that also represent levels of work in a problem-solving group: (1) expressive, (2) technical, (3) inventive, (4) innovative, and (5) emergentive. The mechanisms of drugs and therapy operate primarily at the expressive level to increase spontaneity. The mechanism (process) of skill training will have its main effect at the technical level and brainstorming and similar techniques at the inventive level. For technical or scientific problems the scientific method has the widest range of application, including the possibility of creativity at the emergentive level. For social problems the method of consensus has a similar range. As an example, the process followed by a committee of Quakers and others working on a social problem over a period of one year was described.

A summary of seven steps involved in the creative problem-solving process, especially as it applies to social problems, was given in the form of a flow chart: (1) define problem, (2) collect data from relevant sources, (3) check to see if a solution is already available within the system, (4) if there is no solution available, use the creative problem-solving routines to find a solution at an appropriate level of creativity. (Once a solution is available proceed to Step 5.) (5) test the solution with a pilot project, (6) secure agreement and commitment from those involved, and (7) implement the new system.

Note

1. Guilford's (1975: 39) classification of six types or products of information on "brain produced constructs" show a similar progression from simple to more complex levels of analysis. The six types are: (1) Units, (2) Classes, (3) Relations, (4) Systems, (5) Transformations, and (6) Implications (changes including the redefinition of units and substitutions).

Bibliography

Adelson, Joseph P.
    1975 "Feedback and group development." Small Group Behavior 6 (4): 389-401.
Asch, Solomon E.
    1955 "Opinions and social pressure." Scientific American 193 (5): 31-35.
Back, Kurt W.
    1951 "Influence through social communication." Journal of Abnormal and Social Psychology 46: 9-23.
Bales, Robert F.
    1950 Interaction Process Analysis: A Method for the Study of Small Groups. Cambridge, MA: Addison-Wesley.
    1953 "The equilibrium problem in small groups," pp. 111-161 in T. Parsons, R. F. Bales, and E. A. Shils (eds.) Working Papers in the Theory of Action. Glencoe, IL: Free Press.
    1958 "Task roles and social roles in problem solving groups," pp. 437-447 in E. E. Maccoby, T. M. Newcomb, and E. L. Hartley (eds.) Readings in Social Psychology, 3rd ed. New York: Holt, Rinehart & Winston.
    1968 "Interaction process analysis," pp. 465-471 in D. L. Sills (ed.) International Encyclopedia of the Social Sciences, vol. 7. New York: Macmillan.
    1970 Personality and Interpersonal Behavior. New York: Holt, Rinehart & Winston.
Bales, Robert F., Stephen P. Cohen, and Stephen A. Williamson
    1979 SYMLOG: A System for the Multiple Level Observation of Groups. New York: Free Press.
Bales, Robert F., and Henry Gerbrands
    1948 "The 'Interaction Recorder': An apparatus and check list for sequential content analysis of social interaction." Human Relations 1: 456-463.
Bales, Robert F., Fred L. Strodtbeck, Theodore M. Mills, and Mary E. Roseborough
    1951 "Channels of communication in small groups." American Sociological Review 16: 461-468.
Barron, Frank
    1969 Creative Person and Creative Process. New York: Holt, Rinehart & Winston.
Benne, Kenneth D.
    1964 "History of the T group in the laboratory setting," pp. 80-135 in L. P. Bradford, J. R. Gibb, and K. D. Benne (eds.) T Group Theory and Laboratory Method. New York: John Wiley.

Benne, Kenneth D., and Paul Sheats
    1948 "Functional roles of group members." Journal of Social Issues 4 (2):
          41-49.
Bennis, Warren G., and Herbert A. Shepard
    1956 "A theory of group development." Human Relations 9: 415-437.
Berlew, David E., and William E. LeClere
    1974 "Social intervention in Curacao: A case Study." The Journal of Applied
          Behavioral Science 10 (1): 29-52.
Bernstein, Jeremy
    1973 Einstein. New York: Viking Press.
Bion, W. R.
    1961 Experiences in Groups And Other Papers. New York: Basic Books.
Blake, Robert R.
    1958 "The other person in the situation," pp. 229-242 in R. Tagiuri and L.
          Petrullo (eds.) Person Perception and Interpersonal Behavior. Stanford,
          CA: Stanford University Press.
Blake, Robert R., and Jane S. Mouton
    1969 Building a Dynamic Corporation through Grid Organization Development.
          Reading, MA: Addison-Wesley.
Blatner, Howard A.
    1973 Acting-In. New York: Springer.
Blau, Peter M.
    1960 "A theory of social integration." American Journal of Sociology 63:
          58-69.
    1962 "Patterns of choice in interpersonal relations." American Sociological
          Review 27 (1): 41-55.
    1964 Exchange of Power in Social Life. New York: John Wiley.
    1968 "Social exchange," pp. 452-458 in D. L. Sills (ed.) International Encyclo-
          pedia of the Social Sciences, vol. 7. New York: Macmillan.
Blumberg, Herbert H.
    1973 "Specificity of acquiescence." Journal of Personality Assessment 37:
          479-485.
Blumberg, Herbert H., A. Paul Hare, Valerie Kent, and Martin Davies (eds.)
    1982 Small Groups and Social Interaction. New York: John Wiley.
Borgatta, Edgar F., Arthur S. Couch, and Robert F. Bales
    1954 "Some findings relevant to the great man theory of leadership." American
          Sociological Review 19: 755-759.
Bray, Robert M., Norbert L. Kerr, and Robert S. Atkin
    1978 "Effects of group size, problem difficulty, and sex on group performance
          and member reactions." Journal of Personality and Social Psychology 36
          (11): 1224-1240.
Brinton, Howard H.
    1938 Divine-Human Society. Wallingford, PA: Pendle Hill Publications.
    1943 Guide to Quaker Practice. Wallingford, PA: Pendle Hill Publications.
    1952a Friends for 300 Years. New York: Harper.
    1952b Reaching Decisions. Wallingford, PA: Pendle Hill Publications.
Burke, Kenneth
    1968 "Dramatism," pp. 445-452 in D. L. Sills (ed.) International Encyclopedia
          of the Social Sciences, vol. 7. New York: Macmillan.

Byrne, Donn, and William Griffitt
1973 "Interpersonal attraction." Annual Review of Psychology 24: 317-336.
Carr, L. J.
1929 "Experimental sociology: A preliminary note on theory and method." Social Forces 8: 63-74.
Cartwright, Dorwin, and Alvin Zander (eds.)
1968 Group Dynamics: Research and Theory. 3rd ed. New York: Harper & Row.
Castaneda, Carlos
1968 The Teaching of Don Juan: A Yaqui Way of Knowledge. Berkeley: University of California Press.
Chadwick-Jones, J. K.
1976 Social Exchange Theory: Its Structure and Influence in Social Psychology. London: Academic Press.
Chapple, Eliot D.
1940 "Measuring human relations: An introduction to the study of interaction of individuals." Genetic Psychology Monographs 22: 3-147.
Chase, Stuart
1951 Roads to Agreement. New York: Harper & Row.
Cloyd, Jerry S.
1964 "Patterns of role behavior in informal interaction." Sociometry 27 (2): 161-173.
Cottle, Thomas J.
1976 "An analysis of the phases of development in self-analytic groups," pp. 328-353 in J. J. Loubser, R. C. Baum, and A. Effrat (eds.) Explorations in General Theory in Social Science. New York: Free Press.
Couch, Arthur S.
1960 "Psychological determinants of interpersonal behavior." Ph.D. dissertation, Harvard University.
Coyle, Grace L.
1930 Social Process in Organized Groups. New York: R. R. Smith.
Darley, John M., and Ellen Berscheid
1967 "Increased liking as a result of the anticipation of personal contact." Human Relations 20 (1): 29-40.
Darley, John M., and Bibb Latané
1968 "When will people help in a crisis?" Psychology Today 2 (7): 54-57.
Davis, J.
1975 "The particular theory of exchange." Archives Européenes de Sociologie 16 (2): 151-168.
Davis, James A.
1963 "Structural balance, mechanical solidarity, and interpersonal relations." American Journal of Sociology 68 (4): 444-462.
Davis, James H., Patrick R. Laughlin, and Samuel S. Komorita
1976 "The social psychology of small groups: Cooperative and mixed-motive interaction." Annual Review of Psychology 27: 501-541.
Deutsch, Morton
1954 "Field theory in social psychology," pp. 181-222 in G. Lindzey (ed.) Handbook of Social Psychology. Cambridge, MA: Addison-Wesley.
Deutsch, Morton, and Robert M. Krauss
1960 "The effect of threat upon interpersonal bargaining." Journal of Abnormal and Social Psychology 61 (2): 181-189.

Dodd, Stuart C., and Stefan C. Christopher
    1969 "How to produce consensus: A progress report from project consensus."
         Journal of Human Relations 17 (4): 618-629.
Dunphy, Dexter C.
    1964 "Social change in self-analytic groups." Ph.D. dissertation, Harvard Univer-
         sity.
Effrat, Andrew
    1968 "Editor's introduction." [Applications of Parsonian theory] Sociological
         Inquiry 38 (2): 97-103.
    1976 "Introduction." [Social Change and Development] pp. 662-680 in J. J.
         Loubser, R. C. Baum, A. Effrat, and V. M. Lidz (eds.), Explorations in
         General Theory in Social Science. New York: Free Press.
Emerson, Richard M.
    1976 "Social exchange theory," pp. 335-362 in A. Inkeles, J. Coleman, and N.
         Smelser (eds.) Annual Review of Sociology, vol. 2. Palo Alto, CA: Annual
         Reviews.
Erikson, Erik H.
    1969 Gandhi's Truth: On the Origins of Militant Nonviolence. New York:
         Norton.
Evans, Gary W., and Roger B. Howard
    1973 "Personal space." Psychological Bulletin 80 (4): 334-344.
Farrell, Michael P.
    1976 "Patterns in the development of self-analytic groups." The Journal of
         Applied Behavioral Science 12 (4): 523-542.
Farris, George F.
    1972 "The effect of individual roles on performance in innovative groups." R &
         D Management 31 (2): 23-28.
Feather, Norman T.
    1967 "A structural balance approach to the analysis of communication effects,"
         pp. 100-165 in L. Berkowitz (ed.) Advances in Experimental Social
         Psychology, vol. 3. New York: Academic Press.
Foa, Uriel, and Edna R. Foa
    1974 Societal Structures of the Mind. Springfield, IL: Charles C Thomas.
French, Elizabeth G.
    1956 "Motivation as a variable in work-partner selection." Journal of Abnormal
         and Social Psychology 53: 96-99.
Fromm, Erich
    1959 "The creative attitude," pp. 44-54 in H. H. Anderson (ed.) Creativity and
         Its Cultivation. New York: Harper & Row.
Genovés, Santiago
    1979 The Acali Experiment: Six Women and Five Men on a Raft Across the
         Atlantic. New York: Times Books.
Getzels, Jacob W.
    1975 "Creativity: Prospects and issues," pp. 326-344 in I. A. Taylor and J. W.
         Getzels (eds.) Perspectives in Creativity. Chicago: Aldine.
Goffman, Erving
    1959 The Presentation of Self in Everyday Life. Garden City, NY: Doubleday.
Gordon, William J. J.
    1961 Synectics: The Development of Creative Capacity. New York: Collier
         Books.

Gregg, Richard
   1935   The Power of Nonviolence. Philadelphia: Lippincott.
Guilford, J. P.
   1975   "Creativity: A quarter century of progress," pp. 37-59 in I. A. Taylor and
          J. W. Getzels (eds.) Perspectives in Creativity. Chicago: Aldine.
Gulliver, Philip H.
   1972   Family Herds. Boston: Routledge and Kegan Paul.
Haas, Robert B. (ed.)
   1949   Psychodrama and Sociodrama in American Education. Beacon, NY:
          Beacon House.
Hall, Jay, and W. H. Watson
   1970   "The effects of a normative intervention on group decision-making per-
          formance." Human Relations 23 (4): 299-317.
Hare, A. Paul
   1967   "Small group development in the relay assembly testroom." Sociological
          Inquiry 37 (2): 169-182.
   1968   "Phases in the development of the Bicol Development Planning Board,"
          pp. 29-64 in S. Wells and A. P. Hare (eds.) Studies in Regional Develop-
          ment. Bicol Development Planning Board (Philippines).
   1972   "The nonviolent alternative: Research strategy and preliminary findings,"
          pp. 355-369 in J. F. Short, Jr. and M. E. Wolfgang (eds.) Collective Vio-
          lence. Chicago: Aldine.
   1973a "Group decision by consensus: Reaching unity in the Society of Friends."
          Sociological Inquiry 43 (1): 75-84.
   1973b "Theories of group development and categories for interaction analysis."
          Small Group Behavior 4 (3): 259-304.
   1974   "Rafting across the Atlantic: Social science adrift." Presented at meetings
          of Association for Sociology in Southern Africa, Durban, July.
   1976a "A category system for dramaturgical analysis." Group Psychotherapy,
          Psychodrama and Sociometry 29: 1-14.
   1976b Handbook of Small Group Research (2d ed.). New York: Free Press.
   1977   "Applying the third party approach," pp. 265-287 in A. P. Hare and H. H.
          Blumberg (eds.) Liberation Without Violence. London: Rex Collings.
   1978a "A comparison of Bales' IPA and Parsons' AGIL category systems."
          Journal of Social Psychology 105: 309-310.
   1978b "Images of victims and victimizers in the onset of genocide." Presented at
          Second International Conference on Psychological Stress and Adjustment
          in Time of War and Peace, Jerusalem, June.
   1979   "Moreno, Jacob L.," pp. 537-541 in D. L. Sills (ed.) International Encyclo-
          pedia of the Social Sciences, vol. 18. New York: Macmillan.
   1980a "A dramaturgical analysis of street demonstrations: Washington, D.C.,
          1971 and Cape Town, 1976." Group Psychotherapy, Psychodrama and
          Sociometry 33: 92-120.
   1980b "Consensus versus majority vote: A laboratory experiment." Small Group
          Behavior 11 (2): 131-143.
   1981   "Group size." American Behavioral Scientist 24 (5): 695-708.
Hare, A. Paul, and Herbert H. Blumberg (eds.)
   1968   Nonviolent Direct Action: American Cases: Social-Psychological Analyses.
          Washington, DC: Corpus Books.
   1977   Liberation Without Violence: A Third Party Approach. London: Rex
          Collings.

1980   A Search for Peace and Justice: Reflections of Michael Scott. London: Rex
       Collings.
Hare, A. Paul, Edgar F. Borgatta, and Robert F. Bales (eds.)
1965   Small Groups: Studies in Social Interaction. (Revised edition.) New York:
       Free Press.
Hare, A. Paul, Frank Carney, and Fred Ovsiew
1977   "Youth responds to crisis: Curacao," pp. 220-238 in A. P. Hare and H. H.
       Blumberg (eds.) Liberation Without Violence. London: Rex Collings.
Hare, A. Paul, Herbert M. Kritzer, and Herbert H. Blumberg
1979   "Functional analysis of persuasive interaction in a role-playing experi-
       ment." Journal of Social Psychology 107: 77-88.
Hare, A. Paul, and John Mueller
1979   "Categories for exchange analysis in small groups: With an illustration from
       group psychotherapy." Sociological Inquiry 49 (1): 57-64.
Hare, A. Paul, and Max H. von Broembsen
1979   "The use of consensus at the Constitutional Conference in South West
       Africa." Presented at meetings of the Association for Sociology in
       Southern Africa, Maseru, Lesotho, June.
Hare, A. Paul, and Ellen Wilkinson
1977   "Cyprus: Conflict and its resolution," pp. 239-247 in A. P. Hare and H. H.
       Blumberg (eds.) Liberation Without Violence. London: Rex Collings.
Heider, Fritz
1958   The Psychology of Interpersonal Relations. New York: John Wiley.
Heyerdahl, Thor
1972   The RA Expeditions. New York: New American Library.
Hoffman, Hallock
1968   "The Quaker dialogue," in Center for the Study of Democratic Institutions
       (eds.) The Civilization of the Dialogue 2 (1): 9-12.
Hoffman, L. Richard
1979   The Group Problem-Solving Process: Studies of a Valence Model. New
       York: Praeger.
Hollander, Carl
1969   A Process for Psychodrama Training: The Hollander Psychodrama Curve.
       Littleton, CO: Evergreen Institute Press.
Homans, George C.
1974   Social Behavior: Its Elementary Forms. New York: Harcourt Brace Jovano-
       vich.
Huston, Ted L., and George Levinger
1978   "Interpersonal attraction and relationships." Annual Review of Psychology
       29: 115-156.
Jahoda, Marie
1956   "Psychological issues in civil liberties." American Psychologist 11:
       234-240.
Jennings, Helen H.
1947   "Sociometric differentiation of the psychegroup and the sociogroup."
       Sociometry 10: 71-79.
Kelman, Herbert C.
1958   "Compliance, identification, and internalization: Three processes of
       attitude change." Journal of Conflict Resolution 2: 51-60.

Kiesler, Charles A.
   1969 "Group pressure and conformity," pp. 233-306 in J. Mills (ed.) Experimental Social Psychology. New York: Macmillan.
   1971 The Psychology of Commitment: Experiments Linking Behavior to Belief. New York: Academic Press.
Kiesler, Charles A., and Lee H. Corbin
   1965 "Commitment, attraction, and conformity." Journal of Personality and Social Psychology 2: 890-895.
Kiesler, Charles A., Mark Zanna, and James de Salvo
   1966 "Deviation and conformity: Opinion change as a function of commitment, attraction, and presence of a deviate." Journal of Personality and Social Psychology 3 (4): 458-467.
Komorita, Samuel S., and Jerome M. Chertkoff
   1973 "A bargaining theory of coalition formation." Psychological Review 80 (3): 149-162.
Konečni, Vladimir J., and Ebbe B. Ebbesen
   1975 "Effects of the presence of children on adults' helping behavior and compliance: Two field studies." Journal of Social Psychology 97: 181-193.
Kritzer, Amelia
   1971 "Confrontation behind Selective Service building, April 27, 1971." Haverford College, PA: Nonviolent Action Research Project Field Notes, No. 23.
Kritzer, Herbert M., A. Paul Hare, and Herbert H. Blumberg
   1974 "The general survey: A short form of five personality dimensions." Journal of Personality 86: 165-172.
Kroger, Rolf O.
   1968 "Effects of implicit and explicit task cues upon personality test performance." Journal of Consulting and Clinical Psychology 32: 498.
Leary, Timothy
   1957 Interpersonal Diagnosis of Personality. New York: Ronald.
Leet-Pellegrini, Helena, and Jeffrey Z. Rubin
   1974 "The effects of six bases of power upon compliance, identification, and internalization." Bulletin of the Psychonomic Society 3 (1B): 68-70.
Lewin, Kurt
   1943 "Forces behind food habits and methods of change." Bulletin of the National Research Council 108: 35-65.
Lindsay, John S.
   1976 "On the number and size of subgroups." Human Relations 29 (12): 1103-1114.
Lindzey, Gardner, and Edgar F. Borgatta
   1954 "Sociometric measurement," pp. 405-448 in G. Lindzey (ed.) Handbook of Social Psychology. Cambridge, MA: Addison-Wesley.
Longabaugh, Richard
   1963 "A category system for coding interpersonal behavior as social exchange." Sociometry 26 (3): 319-344.
Loubser, Jan J.
   1976 "Action and experience," pp. 240-263 in J. J. Loubser et al. (eds.) Explorations in General Theory in Social Science. New York: Free Press.

Loubser, Jan J., Rainer C. Baum, Andrew Effrat, and Victor M. Lidz (eds.)
  1976 Explorations in General Theory in Social Science: Essays in Honor of Talcott Parsons. (Vols I and II.) New York: Free Press.

Lundgren, David C.
  1977 "Developmental trends in the emergence of interpersonal issues in T groups." Small Group Behavior 8 (2): 179-200.

MacCannell, Dean
  1973 Nonviolent Action as Theater: A Dramaturgical Analysis of 146 Demonstrations. Haverford College, PA: Nonviolent Action Research Project, Monograph No. 10.

Mann, Richard D., Graham S. Gibbard, and John J. Hartman
  1967 Interpersonal Styles and Group Development. New York: John Wiley.

Marrow, Alfred J.
  1969 The Practical Theorist: The Life Work of Kurt Lewin. New York: Basic Books.

Maslow, Abraham
  1962 Toward a Psychology of Being. Princeton, NJ: Van Nostrand.

Matarazzo, Joseph D., George Saslow, and A. Paul Hare
  1958 "Factor analysis of interview interaction behavior." Journal of Consulting Psychology 22: 419-429.

Matarazzo, Joseph D., George Saslow, and Ruth G. Matarazzo
  1956 "The interaction chronograph as an instrument for objective measurement of interaction patterns during interviews." Journal of Psychology 41: 347-367.

Milgram, Stanley
  1963 "Behavioral study of obedience." Journal of Abnormal and Social Psychology 67 (4): 371-378.

Mills, Theodore M.
  1964 Group Transformation. Englewood Cliffs, NJ: Prentice-Hall.

Miner, Horace M.
  1968 "Community-society continua," pp. 174-180 in D. L. Sills (ed.) International Encyclopedia of the Social Sciences, vol. 3. New York: Macmillan.

Moreno, Jacob L.
  1946 Psychodrama. Volume 1. Beacon, NY: Beacon House.
  1947 The Theatre of Spontaneity. Beacon, NY: Beacon House.
  1953 Who Shall Survive? (Revised edition.) Beacon, NY: Beacon House.

Mulkay, M. J.
  1971 Functionalism, Exchange and Theoretical Strategy. London: Routledge and Kegan Paul.

Nemiroff, Paul M., and Donald C. King
  1975 "Group decision-making performance as influenced by consensus and self-orientation." Human Relations 28 (February): 1-21.

Nesbitt, Paul D.
  1972 "The effectiveness of student canvassers." Journal of Applied Social Psychology 2 (3): 252-258.

Newcomb, Theodore M.
  1953 "An approach to the study of communicative acts." Psychological Review 60: 393-404.
  1963 "Stabilities underlying changes in interpersonal attraction." Journal of Abnormal and Social Psychology 66 (4): 376-386.

Noma, Elliot, and D. Randall Smith
   1978 "SHED: A FORTRAN IV program for the analysis of small group socio-
         metric structure." Behavior Research Methods and Instrumentation 10 (1):
         60-62.
Olmsted, Michael S., and A. Paul Hare
   1978 The Small Group. New York: Random House.
Parsons, Talcott
   1949 Essays in Sociological Theory. (Revised edition.) New York: Free Press.
   1961 "An outline of the social system," pp. 30-79 in T. Parsons et al. (eds.),
         Theories of Society. New York: Free Press.
Parsons, Talcott, Robert F. Bales, and Edward A. Shils
   1953 Working Papers in the Theory of Action. Glencoe, IL: Free Press.
Phillips, John M.
   1972 "Conformity in petition-signing as a function of issue ambiguity." Journal
         of Social Psychology 87: 287-291.
Pollard, F. E., B. E. Pollard, and R.S.W. Pollard
   1949 Democracy and the Quaker Method. London: Bannisdale Press.
Pruitt, Dean G., and Melvin J. Kimmel
   1977 "Twenty years of experimental gaming: Critique, synthesis, and sugges-
         tions for the future." Annual Review of Psychology 28: 363-392.
Rabson, June S.
   1979 Psychodrama: Theory and Method. Cape Town: Department of Sociology,
         University of Cape Town.
Ramsøy, Odd
   1968 "Friendship," pp. 12-17 in D. L. Sills (ed.) International Encyclopedia of
         the Social Sciences, vol. 6. New York: Macmillan.
Redl, Fritz
   1942 "Group emotion and leadership." Psychiatry 5: 573-596.
Riecken, Henry W.
   1952 The Volunteer Work Camp: A Psychological Evaluation. Cambridge, MA:
         Addison-Wesley.
Roethlisberger, Fritz J., and William J. Dickson
   1939 Management and the Worker. Cambridge, MA: Harvard University Press.
Scheff, Thomas J.
   1967 "Toward a sociological model of consensus." American Sociological
         Review 23 (February): 32-45.
Schmuck, Richard, Philip Runkel, and Daniel Langmeyer
   1971 "Theory to guide organizational training in schools." Sociological Inquiry
         41 (2): 183-191.
Schutz, William C.
   1958 FIRO: A Three-Dimensional Theory of Interpersonal Behavior. New York:
         Holt, Rinehart & Winston.
Seashore, Stanley E.
   1954 Group Cohesiveness in the Industrial Work Group. Ann Arbor: University
         of Michigan.
Secord, Paul F., and Carl W. Backman
   1964 "Interpersonal congruency, perceived similarity, and friendship." Socio-
         metry 27 (2): 115-127.
Shambaugh, Philip W.
   1978 "The development of the small group." Human Relations 31 (3): 283-295.

Shaw, Marvin E., and Philip R. Costanzo
    1970 Theories of Social Psychology. New York: McGraw-Hill.
Sherif, Muzafer
    1935 "A study of some social factors in perception." Archives of Psychology 27,
          (187).
Simmel, Georg
    1902- "The number of members as determining the sociological form of the
    1903   group." American Journal of Sociology 8: 1-46, 158-196.
Slater, Philip E.
    1955 "Role differentiation in small groups." American Sociological Review 20:
          300-310.
    1966 Microcosm: Structural, Psychological and Religious Evolution in Groups.
          New York: John Wiley.
Snyder, Eloise C.
    1958 "The Supreme Court as a small group." Social Forces 36: 232-238.
Stanislavski, Constantin
    1961 Creating a Role. New York: Theatre Arts.
Stein, Morris I.
    1974 Stimulating Creativity: Individual Procedures. Vol. 1. New York: Aca-
          demic Press.
    1975 Stimulating Creativity: Group Procedures. Vol. 2. New York: Academic
          Press.
Stock, Dorothy, and Herbert H. Thelen
    1958 Emotional Dynamics and Group Culture. New York: New York University
          Press.
Stogdill, Ralph M.
    1974 Handbook of Leadership: A Survey of Theory and Research. New York:
          Free Press.
Taylor, Frederick W.
    1903 "Group management." Transactions of the American Society of Mechani-
          cal Engineers 24: 1337-1480.
Taylor, Irving A.
    1975 "An emerging view of creative actions," pp. 297-325 in I. A. Taylor and
          J. W. Getzels (eds.) Perspectives in Creativity. Chicago: Aldine.
Thelen, Herbert A.
    1949 "Group dynamics in instruction: Principle of least group size." School
          Review 57: 139-148.
Thibaut, John W. and Harold H. Kelley
    1959 The Social Psychology of Groups. New York: John Wiley.
Triplett, Norman
    1898 "The dynamogenic factors in pacemaking and competition." American
          Journal of Psychology 9: 507-533.
Tuckman, Bruce W.
    1965 "Developmental sequence in small groups." Psychological Bulletin 63 (6):
          384-399.
Tuckman, Bruce W., and Mary A. Jensen
    1977 "Stages of small-group development revisited." Group & Organization
          Studies 2 (4): 419-427.
Turner, Ronny E., and Charles Edgley
    1976 "Death as theater: A dramaturgical analysis of the American funeral."
          Sociology and Social Research 60 (4): 377-392.

Wallach, Michael A., Nathan Kogan, and Daryl J. Bem
    1962 "Group influence on individual risk taking." Journal of Abnormal and Social Psychology 65 (2): 75-86.
Walster, Elaine, G. William Walster, and Ellen Berscheid
    1978 Equity: Theory and Research. Boston: Allyn and Bacon.
White, Ralph K., and Ronald Lippitt
    1960 Autocracy and Democracy. New York: Harper & Row.
Whyte, William F.
    1943 Street Corner Society: The Social Structure of an Italian Slum. Chicago: University of Chicago Press.
Wilder, David A.
    1977 "Perception of groups, size of opposition, and social influence." Journal of Experimental Social Psychology 13 (3): 253-268.
Willis, Richard H., and Yolanda A. Willis
    1970 "Role playing versus deception: An experimental comparison." Journal of Personality and Social Psychology 16: 472-477.

Author Index

Subject Index

About the Author

A. Paul Hare is currently a Professor of Sociology at Ben-Gurion University. Previously he taught at Harvard, Haverford, and the University of Cape Town. Born in 1923 in Washington, D.C., he received academic degrees from Swarthmore, Iowa State (Ames), University of Pennsylvania, and Chicago (Ph.D., 1951). His *Handbook of Small Group Research* is the most extensive review of research on group dynamics and the readings on *Small Groups,* which he co-edited (initially with Borgatta and Bales) has provided basic material in the field through several editions. Three volumes of case studies of nonviolent actions have been edited with Herbert Blumberg. In addition to being the author of many journal articles, he has also been a co-editor of volumes on *South Africa* and *Cooperation in Education.*

Outside the academic environment Paul Hare has been active in applying the insights of group dynamics and the inspiration of the nonviolent movement, most notably as the Deputy Representative for the U.S. Peace Corps in the Philippines (1961-1962), Co-Director of the Antillean Institute of Social Science on Curacao (Summer 1970), Coordinator of the Cyprus Resettlement Project on Cyprus (1973-1974), and Coordinator of Volunteer Service Ambulance Units in South Africa (1976-1980).